THE QUEST TO DISCOVER IF GOD IS REAL

SEARCHING
FOR TRUTH

IN VEGAS, HOLLYWOOD & BETHLEHEM

2/16/2023

STEVE,

THANK Y

EXCELLENT WORK! GOD BLESS
YOU + YOUR FAMILY AS YOU
WALK IN THE LIGHT OF HIS WORD.

"Your MS is an excellent popular case for biblical faith. It is carefully researched, very well written, and stylistically attractive."

~ John Warwick Montgomery,
Lawyer, Professor, Theologian
and Author

THE QUEST TO DISCOVER IF GOD IS REAL

SEARCHING
FOR TRUTH

IN VEGAS, HOLLYWOOD
& BETHLEHEM

GEORGE W. SARRIS

GWS PUBLISHING Grace Will Succeed

Searching for Truth in Vegas, Hollywood & Bethlehem

Copyright © 2023 by George W. Sarris

GWS PUBLISHING Grace Will Succeed

Unless otherwise noted, Scripture quotations are taken from The Holy Bible, New International Version (1984 Edition) copyright © 1973, 1978, 1984 by Biblica, Inc. Used by permission.

ISBN 978-0-9800853-6-5 (Paperback Edition)

For speaking engagements, contact the author at:
George@HeavensDoors.net

Editor, Jack Linn
Interior design, Debbi Stocco
Cover design, Steve Kuhn

For Conrad Koch

Thank you for taking the initiative to talk to me about the greatest news ever announced.

You changed my life!

CONTENTS

INTRODUCTION

WHY ARE WE HERE?

"I went up into space, but I didn't encounter God."

That's from Russian Cosmonaut, Yuri Gargarin, the first human being to journey into outer space and complete one earth orbit on April 12, 1961.[1] There's some debate over his exact words, but the meaning is clear. A short time later, the officially atheist government of the then Soviet Union produced a propaganda poster featuring a cosmonaut floating in space with the slogan, "There Is No God."[2]

Contrast those words with the greeting on Christmas Eve 1968, from Frank Borman, James Lovell and William Anders, the Apollo 8 Astronauts who became the first human beings to leave Earth and orbit the moon. At the time, the broadcast was the most watched television program ever.

"We are now approaching lunar sunrise, and for all the people back on Earth, the crew of

Apollo 8 has a message that we would like to send to you.

"In the beginning God created the heaven and the earth. And the earth was without form, and void; and darkness was upon the face of the deep. And the Spirit of God moved upon the face of the waters.

"And God said, 'Let there be light,' and there was light. And God saw the light, that it was good: and God divided the light from the darkness. And God called the light Day, and the darkness he called Night. And the evening and the morning were the first day.

"And God said, 'Let there be a firmament in the midst of the waters, and let it divide the waters from the waters.' And God made the firmament, and divided the waters which were under the firmament from the waters which were above the firmament, and it was so. And God called the firmament Heaven. And the evening and the morning were the second day." [3]

Should Cosmonauts or Astronauts who travel into space expect to encounter some kind of divine Being, perhaps with a long, white beard dressed in a flowing robe and seated on a throne judging the universe? Probably not. Should they expect to see clear evidence of a finely tuned universe brought into existence by an intelligent Designer? Much more likely.

WHERE DID IT ALL COME FROM?

The universe we live in is really big, and it's really complex.

The galaxy we call the Milky Way where Earth is situated is estimated to contain at least 100 billion stars, with the observable universe containing at least 100 billion galaxies. If the number of stars in all those other galaxies is similar to that of the Milky Way, there is an estimated 70 billion trillion (or 70 sextillion) stars in the observable universe. That amounts to about 10 times more stars than there are grains of sand on all the seashores of all the Earth.[4] And, as far as we can tell, the laws of nature that operate consistently on Earth and in our solar system also operate consistently throughout the rest of the universe.[5]

So how did all of this come about? Did it just happen? Or was all of what we see brought into being by a very intelligent, very powerful and very skillful Designer?

Very few people actually believe that everything that exists came from absolutely *nothing*. No matter. No energy. Nothing.

However, a frequent explanation for where everything came from is that the Creation created itself out of something. What we see ultimately came from some form of energy that makes up the natural, material universe. In many ways, this is the dominant view of our culture today embodied in the Theory of Evolution and in the more philosophical view of many who believe that the material universe itself is an impersonal life force with a consciousness of its own.

VEGAS

The Theory of Evolution, or what one friend refers to as the *Las Vegas Theory of Origins* because of its dependence on chance, begins with the assumption that energy has always existed in the universe in some form or another. In its current formulation, it's suggested that the *something* that has always existed began as some kind of atom or "Cosmic Egg" that subsequently exploded into everything in what is often called the Big Bang.

After the explosion, the unguided mass or energy that existed organized itself into elements. The elements then reorganized themselves into chemicals and chemical processes ... which then developed into living, unconscious organisms ... that developed into living, conscious organisms ... and ultimately into living, conscious, reasoning organisms. All of this resulted from random happenings with nothing but chance directing the process.

HOLLYWOOD

While holding views that are in many ways totally opposite those held in the so-called scientific community, people who believe that the universe is actually an impersonal life force or energy that transforms and reincarnates itself over time actually agree with the natural explanation of origins that the Creation created itself. My friend calls this the *Hollywood Theory of Origins* because of its relationship to the Force of *Star Wars.*

This belief has its roots in Eastern religions such as Hinduism and Buddhism, became popular during the counterculture movement of the 1960s with its interest in Transcendental Meditation, and saw its influence on the culture grow with the New Age movement in the 1970s and 1980s.

There is no standard set of beliefs that all its adherents hold to. However, similar to the Theory of Evolution, a central tenet held by most who believe in this all-pervasive life force is that nothing exists outside the material universe. This force or energy has always existed and will always exist. As it relates to the origin and development of all things, instead of chance directing everything, the universe directs itself.

BETHLEHEM

The alternative to the idea that everything ultimately came from some form of pre-existing matter or energy is that a Creator existing outside the natural, material universe brought all of what we see into existence. The *size* of the universe suggests that this Creator has phenomenal power. The *complexity* of the universe suggests that this Creator has phenomenal skill and intelligence.

This is, of course, the Biblical view which dominated Western culture until the early 20th century, as can be seen by the simple fact that we use the word "creation" to describe what the universe is. This view is what my friend refers to as the *Bethlehem Theory of Origins*. The heavens and the earth didn't just happen. They were brought into existence by a sovereign Creator.

So, which is true? Did the creation create itself? Or did a Creator bring all of what we see into existence? How we answer those questions is something we should all seriously consider because the implications actually have an impact on how we conduct ourselves in life.

WHAT'S THE BIG DEAL?

The most important implication of the Theory of Evolution is that people are ultimately *insignificant.*

If we are simply a chance mixing of elements which exist as human beings today and tomorrow return to dust with nothing else in the future, then our importance as individuals is really no greater than that of a rock. Or a sea urchin. An evolutionist must view himself or herself as nothing more than an animal in a certain stage of development. We may influence the course of life in some small degree while we are alive, but ultimately we are simply a relatively meaningless blip in the long eons of history which itself is relatively meaningless since nothing really has a purpose anyway. In fact, the rock may be more significant than we are since it will surely outlast us, and, depending on its size and location, may have more influence on what happens in the course of history than we do.

Similarly, those who seek to become one with the universe must view themselves as *nothings*. If they are correct in their philosophical musings about the universe and life, then our ultimate goal is to lose our individual identities. By losing our individuality, "You" and "I" really cease to exist. We become nothing.

By contrast, the most important implication of the view that God created the heavens and the earth, at least as it is understood from a Biblical context, is that each individual has great significance. Every one of us has been made in the image of God. We are *not* simply a chance mixing of elements, and we *do* have a unique purpose for why we are here. Death is not the end of existence, but the gateway into life. Instead of seeking a state in the here and now where we cease to exist as individuals, our true personalities are enlivened and we are free to become the unique persons we were made to be.

The writer of the Biblical book of Ecclesiastes was correct when he said that "under the sun," where life exists without reference to a divine Creator, everything is meaningless – a chasing after the wind.[6] For a person who believes in God, however, life "under heaven," where it is lived in accord with the plans and purposes of the divine Creator, has great meaning and purpose.

ONE SMALL STEP ... ONE GIANT LEAP

On the evening of the day after my 21st birthday, I was in my uncle's restaurant. Patrons and workers alike were crowded around a small television set watching a black and white image of a truly historic event.

At 10:56 PM Eastern Time on July 20, 1969, Neil Armstrong emerged from the lunar capsule of the Apollo 11 space flight to become the first human being ever to set foot on the moon. Nineteen minutes later, Edwin "Buzz" Aldrin became the second person to step onto the moon's surface.

After their successful landing, Aldrin radioed to Earth,

"This is the LM pilot. I'd like to take this opportunity to ask every person listening in, whoever and wherever they may be, to pause for a moment and contemplate the events of the past few hours and to give thanks in his or her own way."

Using a kit given to him by his pastor, he then took communion privately. He later said,

"... at the time, I could think of no better way to acknowledge the enormity of the Apollo 11 experience than by giving thanks to God."[7]

1

DID THE CREATION CREATE ITSELF?

*"I don't believe in God as I don't
believe in Mother Goose."*

So said Clarence Darrow, the defense lawyer in what is one of the most famous and fascinating court trials in all of history.[8] In July 1925, a high school teacher in Dayton, Tennessee named John T. Scopes was tried on charges that he had violated a Tennessee law that made it illegal to teach evolution.

The Scopes Monkey Trial, as it was called then and since, drew worldwide attention. The front pages of *The New York Times*, *The Baltimore Sun* and other major newspapers from around the country were dominated by the case for days. More than 200 reporters from across the US, and even two journalists who sailed across the ocean all the way from London covered the trial. At a time when 82% of Americans listened regularly to the radio, it was the first US news story to be broadcast nationally, becoming a one-way social media site for its time with tremendous impact on its listeners.

The ACLU had offered to defend anyone accused of teaching evolution in violation of the recently passed law, and the city of Dayton saw this as an opportunity to attract publicity for the town. But what began as a publicity stunt quickly became a circus. Because of the summer heat and the thousands of spectators flocking to the scene, the trial was moved outside where preachers set up revival tents along the city's main street, and carnival barkers exhibited two chimpanzees and a supposed "missing link."[9] Street vendors sold Bibles, toy monkeys, hot dogs and lemonade.

Thirty years after the trial, it became the subject of a major Broadway play, *Inherit the Wind*. Five years after that, it was made into a major motion picture starring big name actors of the time, including Spencer Tracy, Frederic March and Gene Kelly. Television adaptations in 1965, 1988 and 1999 featured A-List actors including Jason Robards, George C. Scott, Jack Lemmon and Kirk Douglas. In 2023, bestselling author Gregg Jarrett released, *The Trial of the Century*, detailing the Scopes Trial and its significance.

At the trial, two famous lawyers agreed to represent the two sides. William Jennings Bryan who had been Secretary of State and the Democratic Party's nominee for President three times argued for the prosecution, and Clarence Darrow, a big name Chicago criminal lawyer, led the defense.

In a daring and shrewd move, Darrow effectively turned the defense into the prosecution by calling Bryan to take the witness stand, where he was publicly humiliated in the cross-examination. Although Darrow actually lost the battle (his client was convicted and fined $100), he clearly won the war. Within a short period of time, the teaching of Evolution in public school classrooms was not only allowed, it completely supplanted the teaching of Creation as the only acceptable scientific theory of origins.

Today, it's almost impossible to go to a museum or aquarium, watch a nature documentary, take a tour of a national park, or read a newspaper or magazine article about some scientific discovery without hearing that the universe and life evolved over billions of years from non-living chemicals ... to single-celled organisms ... to the complex life forms that make up life today.

The news coverage and media productions overwhelmingly cast those who stood for Creation as foolish, backward hillbillies. In the last century, it has been one of the primary reasons why people have chosen to abandon their faith to pursue other theological or philosophical speculations.

LAS VEGAS THEORY OF ORIGINS

In the last few decades, however, the tide has begun to turn and Evolution has had to face cross-examination on the witness stand.

An increasing number of scientists have begun to question the evidence and underlying assumptions behind the teaching of Evolution. They have written books, conducted seminars, engaged in Creation/Evolution debates on college campuses, been interviewed on radio and television talk shows, and testified in court rooms challenging the validity of Evolution on scientific grounds. Their study of the issues has led them to conclude that Evolution is a weakly supported theory that does not hold up under careful scrutiny, and that the supernatural view of Creation by an intelligent Designer fits the facts far better.[10]

In a way similar to how mainstream journalists maligned and ridiculed the participants in the original Scopes Trial, these scientists today are often treated in the popular media, academia and online as backward, incompetent, and out-of-touch with reality. However, even one website that is openly hostile to the idea of scientific creation still lists 152 creationist scientists who they considered "qualified" to address the issues involved.[11]

There are three primary reasons why these scientists have abandoned the Theory of Evolution, based as it is on random chance occurrences, and now favor Creation by an intelligent Designer as the probable origin of all things.

FIRST, EVOLUTION IS CONTRARY TO THE ESTABLISHED LAWS OF SCIENCE

Science deals with what can be observed and tested. The role of science as it relates to the study of origins is really limited to trying to answer the question, "*Could it happen?*" Are there laws of physics or chemistry or some other discipline which rule out one option as a possibility? As a matter of fact, there are.

Every observation that has ever been made and all the scientific studies that have ever been undertaken support what is known as the Law of Increasing Entropy. It's not a "Law" because some governing board of scientists got together, debated the various issues involved, and decided that this is the way things ought to be. It's called a "Law" because *every* credible observation and *every* credible scientific study ever conducted has concluded that this Law accurately describes what is, in fact, true.

This established Law of science measures the amount of *useable* energy in any system, and basically states that the natural tendency of any system is toward disorder. [12]

Energy is useable when it's concentrated. When it's dissipated, it's no longer available to be used. The sun, for example, is a very large, highly concentrated source of energy. As such, its energy can be used to provide light and heat to our entire world. It's the source of energy for photosynthesis in plants, and it can be harnessed by solar energy devices to heat water, power devices, and generate electricity.

This scientific Law, however, points to the fact that the sun will someday burn out. Its energy will eventually be dissipated and our solar system will experience what some have called a heat death. The actual energy of the sun will still be in existence in the form of a low, evenly distributed temperature throughout the universe. However, since it is not concentrated, that energy will not be able to be harnessed and used.

Put plainly, the Law of Increasing Entropy notes that things always run down, wear out or break down with time. The car you drive will eventually stop running and need to be replaced. The body you inhabit will eventually breathe its last breath and turn to dust. All machines will someday break down. All living organisms will someday die. Without the addition of intelligently directed energy, nothing tends toward a more ordered or complex state.

I was riding the subway in New York City some time ago and saw an interesting billboard for a technical trade school that, perhaps unknowingly, captured the essence of what the Entropy Law teaches. The billboard simply read,

"Things Break ... that's why skilled technicians will always be in demand."

Machines don't naturally work better over time. They break. They don't naturally fix themselves. They need skillful technicians to fix them.

In complete contrast to this, Evolution teaches that matter and organisms, if given enough time, become more ordered and more complex *without* the addition of intelligently directed energy. What began as nothing, suddenly exploded into something, and eventually developed, on its own, into everything.

More specifically, "nothing" exploded to become hydrogen gas (the only element in existence after the theorized Big Bang). This hydrogen gas then slowly compacted and organized itself into stars which, like our sun, are composed of hydrogen, helium and other elements. These stars later exploded and reorganized themselves into planets, which then cooled down and reorganized their atomic structures into the material elements. The material elements then mixed together and reorganized into living cells, which later grew and organized themselves into extraordinarily complex living creatures.

This proposed phenomenal increase in order and complexity over time that is the heart of Evolution is directly contradicted by this scientific Law. The direction for the flow of complexity is wrong. The true direction of every system is toward disorder, not toward increased order and complexity.

SECOND, EVOLUTION IS CONTRARY TO PAST AND CURRENT OBSERVATION

History deals with what happened in the past. It relies on the study of historical documents which contain the observations of those who lived before the present, and on the study of the remains of things left over from the past. As it relates to the study of origins, it seeks to answer the question, "*Did* something that is claimed to be true in the past actually happen?" That means looking at the fossil record.

Contrary to Evolution, observation of life from the past by means of the fossil record as well as current observation and testing of living organisms in the present show that living things always reproduce in line with the kind of creatures they are. Individual organisms often show significant variations in size, color, and certain features to be sure. But dogs are always dogs, cats are always cats, and fruit flies are always fruit flies.[13]

While evolutionists often point to the fossil record

as evidence of Evolution taking place in the past, what they don't point out is that all of the fossils ever discovered are of creatures with fully formed and functional features. This is true of extinct species as well as currently existing species. In actual fact, there is not simply a missing link, there are missing links at every significant transitional point. [14]

For example, there are absolutely no forms of life in the fossil record or in the present world between single-celled creatures and complex invertebrates such as jellyfish, worms, sea urchins, and sponges. There are also no forms of life in the fossil record or in the present world between creatures with no backbone and creatures with a backbone. Or between non-flying insects and flying insects. Or between the major fish classes. Or between fish and mammals. Or dogs and cats, or horses and elephants, right on up to man. At every point, right from the start, worms are worms, dragonflies are dragonflies, angel fish are angel fish, and cows are cows.

As in any area of study, there are facts, and there are interpretations of those facts. Almost all of the evidence presented to support Evolution is based on similarities between different kinds of plants and animals. Because various living organisms have similar structures, evolutionists have argued that one must have evolved into the other.

A completely different explanation, however, and one that rings true with our observations of how things actually work in the real world, is that the similar structures were designed specifically by an intelligent Designer for similar purposes. The fossil record is very much like a junk yard containing the remains of once active and functioning mechanisms. One could apply evolutionary presuppositions to a vehicle junk yard and say that because they all have wheels, what began as a unicycle, slowly evolved on its own into a bicycle, then a tricycle, later a VW Bug, a Fiat Spider, a Chevrolet Corvette, a Cadillac limousine and eventually a BMW, which, according to its current advertising slogan, is the "Ultimate Driving Machine!" At certain critical points, offshoots evolved into airplanes, trucks and boats.

One could also conclude from the evidence that each type of vehicle was purposely designed by intelligent designers who understood that it was wise to use similar parts to perform similar functions. The key to understanding the truth about junk yards is the realization that complex mechanisms don't just happen.

THIRD, EVOLUTION DOESN'T MAKE SENSE THEORETICALLY

There is no advantage to an organism having only part of an eye, or part of an ear, or part of an internal organ. Half a wing, or wings with solid bones, or part feathers/part scales, part lungs/part gills, part legs/part flippers would not help organisms survive. Rather, they would lead quickly to that organism's death. If a system is not fully functional from the start, it's a hindrance to an organism's survival, not a benefit. Yet, Evolution teaches that complex, interrelated systems gradually developed.

A wonderful example of this is the Nudibranch Sea Slug.[15] The meal of choice for sea slugs is sea anemones. The problem is that sea anemones are covered with tiny, poisonous stinging cells which burst and send out their poison at the slightest touch. Sea slugs, however, have the amazing ability to swallow the stinging cells without bursting them. Then, inside a sea slug's stomach, moving hairs send the stinging cells to tiny tubes which transport them up to waving spurs on its back. The sea slugs then use these poisonous cells as weapons against the fish which attack them.

A sea slug with only part of the system in place for eating sea anemones would be in very great danger. If the sea slug were not able to swallow the sea anemone without bursting the poisonous stinging cells, it would die when it tried to eat one. If it did not have a system in place in its stomach to move the stinging cells along without bursting them, it would die after it ate the sea anemone. If it didn't have the ability to store and fire the stinging cells from the waving spurs on its back, it would die as a result of being eaten by a predator.

If any of the numerous steps along the way were not entirely in place when the sea slug began to eat sea anemones, the sea slug would be dead meat.

MONKEYS STILL PLAY A ROLE

Even after the Scopes Monkey Trial, monkeys have continued to play a role in the creation/evolution debate, primarily as one of the most often used arguments in support of the idea that chance, if given enough time, is a sufficient mechanism for explaining the origin of all things. The argument goes something like this:

> "Isn't it possible that millions of monkeys typing on millions of typewriters for millions of years would produce a copy of the Encyclopedia Britannica?"

The actual answer to that question is, "No," in part because of the destructive forces that would be at work throughout the process.

For example, the monkeys would die, the typewriters would break, and the paper being typed on would disintegrate over the postulated millions-of-years time frame. The same would be true of the destructive forces at work destroying the supposed building blocks of life long before they would be able to come together to form any kind of living organism.[16]

WHAT IS EVOLUTION, REALLY?

Many scientists and a great number of people have never really questioned the evolutionary assumptions they were taught in school, in part because those assumptions are communicated so often and in so many ways in books and magazines, on television and in museums that people just assume that it must be true. But it's important to keep in mind that Evolution is only a *theory*.

One website lists 27 different definitions for what a theory is, and allows visitors to the site to vote on the one they believe is the best. The definition at the top of the list?

An unproven concept.[17]

2

WHAT HAPPENED 'IN THE BEGINNING'?

"It's a power that Jedi have that lets them control people ... and make things float."

That's what Rey said in *Star Wars* Episode VIII – *The Last Jedi* to a much older and ill-tempered Luke Skywalker in response to his question asking her what she knew about the Force. He quickly explained that she was completely wrong, but Rey's response actually illustrates the fact that different people have very different ideas about what the *Star Wars* Force really is.

The *Star Wars* film series debuted in only 32 theaters when its first film came out in 1977, but it soon became a worldwide pop-culture phenomenon that expanded to include other films, television series, video games, novels, comic books, and theme park attractions. The franchise is estimated to be worth $70 billion, and is currently the fifth-highest-grossing media franchise of all time.[18]

The idea of the "Force" as a popular way of combining religion and science quickly caught on. In 2005, the phrase "May the Force be with you" was chosen as number 8 in a list of the top 100 best movie quotations in American cinema.[19] May 4th has become Star Wars Day for some as they greet one another with, "May the Fourth be with you."

So what is the Force? The creator of the *Star Wars* series, George Lucas, once explained,

> "The act of living generates a force field, an energy. That energy surrounds us; when we die, that energy joins with all the other energy. There is a giant mass of energy in the universe that has a good side and a bad side. We are part of the Force because we generate the power that makes the Force live. When we die, we become part of that Force, so we never really die; we continue as part of the Force."[20]

Obi-Wan Kenobi described it more simply in the first film as

> "… an energy field created by all living things. It surrounds us and penetrates us. It binds the galaxy together."[21]

Over the course of the nine films, ideas related to the Force changed somewhat as different directors and writers added their ideas, but the general idea resembles a number of real-world religions, including the focus on a unifying energy in the universe in Hinduism and the conflict between good and evil in Zoroastrianism.

HOLLYWOOD THEORY OF ORIGINS

We've noted that "chance" is not a sufficient mechanism to adequately explain the incredible increase in order and complexity we see in the natural world around us. But could something like the *Star Wars* Force that is created by all living things and binds our galaxy together with its light and dark sides actually be the something that has always existed that everything ultimately came from?

That is definitely a possibility, and one of the most important Laws of science actually lends a degree of credibility to it. The Law of the Conservation of Energy states that the amount of energy existing in any closed system remains constant over time. It's often represented by the phrase, "Energy can neither be created nor destroyed, it can only be transformed."[22]

What that means in practical terms is that as we look forward in time, the *total amount* of energy existing in the universe always remains the same. The same amount of energy exists today as has ever existed in the past, and will ever exist in the future. We can't create it. We can't ultimately destroy it. We can only transform it from one form to another.

So maybe the unifying energy of the Force has actually been with us forever and, as Obi-Wan said, it's what binds the universe together. The only problem is that the Conservation Law, when looked at alongside the Entropy Law we discussed earlier, indicates that the universe definitely did have a beginning.

GOING BACK ... TO THE BEGINNING

When these two Laws of science are taken together, we learn that the *total amount* of energy existing in the universe remains the same whether we go forward or backward in time. However, that is not the case with the amount of *useable* energy existing in the universe. If we were to go forward in time, the amount of useable energy available to us would decrease. In AD 5000, for example, there will actually be less useable energy in the universe than there is today.

However, if we were to go *back* in time, the amount of useable energy would increase. There was more *useable* energy in a more ordered state in the year 5000 BC than exists today.

So the question is: How far back can we go?

Since it's impossible to have more useable energy than energy in existence, we can only go back to the point when those two forms of energy were exactly the same. We could only go back to the point when *all* of the existing energy was useable and ordered. When those two forms of energy were exactly the same, something major occurred.

At that precise moment, the universe began. And when it began, it was in a highly ordered, complex state.

At that precise moment, time began.

And at that precise moment, the physical laws that govern our universe began.

At some specific point in the distant past, the natural, material universe came into being. The theorized energy field created by all living things that binds the galaxy together had a beginning. The Force is *not* the something that has always existed that everything came from, which leads us to the third possibility – creation by an intelligent Designer.

THE BETHLEHEM THEORY OF ORIGINS

The fundamental observations of science, philosophy and everyday observation that every effect must have a sufficient cause and every design must have a designer certainly indicate that the concept of creation by an intelligent Creator is within the realm of possibility, if not probability.

As builders and artisans create buildings, bridges, cars, trucks, tools and works of art that are separate from themselves, so it is very reasonable that an extremely powerful, extremely intelligent and transcendent Being brought the universe with its physical laws and characteristics into existence as an entity separate and distinct from itself. And as the works of builders and artisans are stamped with signs of their character and skill, so we would expect that the universe would be stamped with signs of the character and skill of the One who designed it.

CREATION BY AN INTELLIGENT DESIGNER IS DIRECTLY SUPPORTED BY THE ESTABLISHED LAWS OF SCIENCE, INCLUDING THE EXCEPTIONS

The very fact that there are natural laws which govern the universe suggests strongly that the universe is actually governed, rather than the product of chance. In fact, we call what is out there a "universe" specifically because there are universal laws that consistently apply throughout. We are able to send space probes to various planets precisely because the same physical laws that operate everywhere on earth also operate, as far as we can tell, everywhere in space.

What is most interesting, however, is a look at the exceptions to various laws that indicate a guiding Hand behind them.

For example, the scientific laws relating to electromagnetic attraction point out clearly that unlike charges attract and like charges repel ... *except* in the nucleus of an atom, the building block for everything in the material universe. For some reason still not fully understood, like-charged protons hold together. They do *not* repel!

Scientists describe this as the "strong nuclear force" which overcomes the electromagnetic force and prevents the electrical repulsion of protons from blowing the nucleus apart.[23] If it were not for this exception, *everything* would explode. We wouldn't have stars, planets, rocks, animals, people or anything else in the "creation."

The Bible actually alludes to this in a letter written by the apostle Paul to the Colossian Christians.

"For by Him all things were created: things in heaven and on earth, visible and invisible ... He is before all things, and *in Him all things hold together.*"[24]

Another example of a strategic exception would be physical laws relating to expansion and contraction. As materials get hotter, they expand. As they get colder, they contract ... *except* in the case of the most abundant material on earth – water!

Like all substances, water becomes more dense when it is cooled. However, unlike almost all other substances, when water reaches 4 degrees C, it suddenly stops becoming more dense and begins to expand. When it turns to ice, it floats. It also freezes from the top down, instead of from the bottom up.

If this were not the case, lakes in cold climates would freeze, killing all the fish and other forms of life in the lake. The ice on the surface also shields and insulates the lakes from the cold temperatures outside, allowing the water underneath to stay liquid and maintain a temperature adequate for life in the lake to survive.[25]

Throughout the natural world, there are exceptions to general rules of what we would expect in just the areas necessary for life to exist.

CREATION BY AN INTELLIGENT DESIGNER IS SUPPORTED BY ALL PAST AND CURRENT OBSERVATION

As we saw when we looked at Evolution, organisms always reproduce according to their kinds. All of nature also displays a phenomenal degree of complexity that is actually boggling to the mind, suggesting very strongly that a phenomenal intelligence designed it.

If Neil Armstrong, after taking his one small step for man, suddenly took one giant leap for mankind and reported on his radio to earth that he had discovered drawings of a leaf, along with a camera, a pump, and a laptop computer in a lunar cave, would he have assumed that what he found "just happened" to form themselves from materials existing on the moon? Or would he have concluded that he had discovered evidence that someone else had actually gotten there first?

The obvious answer is that he would have discovered evidence that intelligent beings had already been there. Why? Because each of the things he saw had a design. The parts were all interrelated for some special purpose.

The way the colors and lines are laid out on drawings, and the way the various parts of cameras, pumps, and computers are connected to one another indicates that there is a reason behind why they are put together in just that way. The higher the degree of complexity, the more probable the conclusion that they were designed by an intelligent being. And as the complexity of the design increases, it is evidence of a more mature skill or intelligence.

For example, if one of the leaf drawings looked like it had been made by a child, while another was a very detailed botanical illustration, it could lead to the additional conclusion that astronaut Armstrong had discovered evidence that a family with a scientist and a child were living in the cave.

If pictures of leaves drawn by children and botanists provide clear evidence that they are designed by intelligent beings, how much more impressed should we be that there is an Intelligence behind a real leaf, with its complex system of photosynthesis that enables it to actually transform chemicals with the aid of the sun's light?

Or if we are convinced that a camera has been purposefully designed by some intelligent designer, how much more impressed should we be by the design, and the Designer, of the human eye, with its supersensitive light meter, immediate automatic focusing, and full-color instantaneous reproduction?

If we think a water pump shows evidence that it has been thoughtfully put together, how much more readily should we conclude that the self repairing pump we call the heart, which can pump 100,000 times a day for 70 years or more without shutting down for maintenance or repair has been thoughtfully put together?

And if we are forced by the complexity of a laptop computer to conclude that it was not produced by chance but by individuals or groups of individuals with a high degree of intelligence, how much more readily should we conclude that our own brains, which sort, store, and act upon electrical signals from 200,000 living thermometer cells, 500,000 pressure sensing cells, 3 or 4 million pain sensing cells, plus signals from our eyes, ears, nose, and areas sensitive to taste and touch could not have been produced by chance, but are evidence of a Designer with a very high degree of intelligence?

As a carrier of information, the DNA molecule is 45 trillion times more efficient than a computer chip which was designed by teams of designers![26] And unlike machines designed by man, living organisms are self-repairing and self-replicating, with each part perfectly designed for the function it is to perform. As far as we can determine, the design cannot be improved.

The difference between what is found in nature and what is man-made is seen most clearly when each is placed under a microscope. The closer you look at what is man-made, the more you see its *imperfections*. The closer you look at something in nature, the more impressed you are with its *intricate complexity*!

One friend who had knee-replacement surgery commented as he was learning to walk again, "It's good. But the replacement knee doesn't come close to the original!" Another friend once asked, "How would you design a better squirrel?"

CREATION BY AN INTELLIGENT DESIGNER MAKES SENSE THEORETICALLY

Fully designed and functioning complex systems are very useful. But partly designed or partly functioning systems are not. The parts in watches, cars, computers, calculators, pumps, telephones, airplanes, etc. all need to be in place at the same time and working properly for the item to operate correctly and efficiently. Anyone who owns an automobile knows from experience that if even a small part malfunctions, the entire car just sits there.

There are countless numbers of examples of phenomenally intricate systems that make up every living organism. It makes sense to believe that they were purposefully designed. It doesn't make sense to think that they "just happened."

One example is the Bombardier Beetle. This tiny creature has a magnificent defense system that almost defies imagination. When a predator decides to approach this ½ inch long beetle and invite him for lunch, it turns quickly around and literally fires hot, corrosive gasses heated to near 212 degrees Fahrenheit from a little cannon in its rear.

In order to be able to do this, the Bombardier Beetle has special storage chambers for chemicals that will explode when combined, a special inhibitor that prevents the chemicals from exploding while inside the little beetle, an anti-inhibitor and special enzymes which operate as a catalyst to make the chemical reaction move along very rapidly when the time is right, valves and combustion tubes, and a marvelously designed set of muscles to direct the explosion in the right direction when the predator approaches. Everything must work perfectly, or the Bombardier Beetle gets eaten. Having the complete system in place argues powerfully that it was purposefully designed.[27]

The *Bethlehem Theory of Origins* – that the creation has a Creator is supported by all the established laws of science. It is supported by all past and current observation. And it makes sense theoretically.

THE REAL DIFFERENCE

The study of origins is not strictly a scientific issue. It actually deals with the fields of history and philosophy, as well. Science deals with what can be observed at present and measured or tested, whereas the origin of all things occurred in the unobservable past.

People often claim that they reject Creation by an intelligent Designer because the scientific or historic evidence demands it. In reality, some may have chosen philosophically to reject Creation because they reject the idea of a Creator. For to believe in a Creator requires an adherence to the Creator's moral standards and standards of conduct.

I've often wondered why things that exist in nature only vaguely resemble our designed machines. The wings of a bird, for example, as compared to the wings of an airplane. Or the eye of an eagle as compared to a Nikon camera. I've concluded that they look so different because our machines are of such inferior quality!

I can imagine a conversation between two hummingbirds looking at a new, sophisticated helicopter.

"It's certainly big. And it can move up and down and make turns a lot better than a regular airplane. So, hey, I'd give it an 'A' for effort!"

3

WHAT IS GOD LIKE?

"god is not Great!"

That was not only the sentiment of the self described "anti-theist" Christopher Hitchens for most of his life, it became the title of his 2007 best-selling book.

Hitchens was a British born author, journalist and literary critic noted for his biting wit and eloquent writing style. He authored 11 books, co-authored six more and had five collections of essays published. He was a regular contributor to major periodicals including *Newsday, Vanity Fair* and *Atlantic Monthly,* and a frequent guest on cable TV shows.[28]

Hitchens believed that a person could be an atheist and wish that belief in God were correct. However, an *anti-theist* like himself "is someone who is relieved that there's no evidence for such an assertion."[29] When asked what he considered to be the "axis of evil" in this world, he pointed to the three leading monotheisms – Christianity, Judaism and Islam. In his book, he expanded his criticisms to include all organized religions, concluding that they are the main source of hatred in the world.

god is not Great received mixed reviews, ranging from praise for his piercing writing style,

> "Hitchens has nothing new to say, although it must be acknowledged that he says it exceptionally well"[30]

to accusations of intellectual and moral shabbiness,

> "...in presenting the secular rationalist versus the religious fanatic, he obscures the fact that the greatest slaughters of human history, by far, were not the result of religious wars, but the result of secular or non-religious ideologies. Stalin, Hitler, Mao slaughtered more human beings than all the religious wars of history by a ten fold factor."[31]

Hitchens was a heavy smoker and drinker throughout his life, and died of esophageal cancer at the age of 62. His wit came out even after being diagnosed with cancer, telling one interviewer, "No evidence or argument has yet been presented which would change my mind. But I like surprises."[32]

GOOD, BAD OR INDIFFERENT?

Contrary to what Christopher Hitchens believed, the phenomenal degree of intelligence required to design the intricately complex existence in which we live does argue persuasively that an intelligent Designer created it. If we add to that fact the nature of human beings as personal beings with emotions, hopes, and longings of the heart, it's all the more probable that the Creator is a Person. But Hitchens' challenge still must be addressed. What is this God like?

Is He good? Or bad? Or a combination of the two?

Is He interested and involved in the lives of men and women today? Or is He more like a Divine Watchmaker who designed and built an incredible timepiece, wound it up, and then let it run on its own while He went off to do something else?

Is God a moral Being with standards of right and wrong? Or does He allow each of us to decide what is "right" for ourselves?

Has God ever clearly communicated to His creation anything about who He is or what He has done?

THAT STILL, SMALL VOICE

In addition to the fact that the creation itself speaks volumes about the Creator's awesome power and intelligence, there is another universal reality that gives us a definite clue as to what this Creator is like.

All human beings on this earth have a still, small voice inside our hearts that talks to us about what we should and should not do. We call it the voice of conscience. The dictionary defines conscience as,

"The sense or consciousness of the moral goodness or blameworthiness of one's own conduct, intentions, or character together with a feeling of obligation to do right or be good."

It's the inherent sense in all of us that some things are right and some things are wrong, along with a feeling that we are obligated to do what is right.

The reason this has bearing on the issue before us is that it indicates clearly that there's a moral quality to the universe and life. Something inside us prompts us to do good, and then cheers us on by giving us a sense of well-being when we do it. It also warns us not to do wrong, and condemns us in the form of guilt when we choose to defy its voice.

As we all know from personal experience, our consciences can be resisted and even dulled. A Native American proverb explains that the conscience is like a square block inside your heart. When you do something wrong, the block turns, the corners dig in, and it hurts. But if it's turned too often, the corners wear down and it doesn't hurt so much.

The conscience can certainly be scarred and even

twisted, but it remains there nevertheless. The fact that it is there universally is a strong indication that there is a moral Voice behind the creation. The fact that our consciences universally prompt us to do what is "right" is a strong indication that the One who created that voice within us is good.

What we can learn from a study of the creation around us and the voice of conscience within us, however, is limited to the fact that the Creator has awesome power and intelligence, and He is in some way "good." But what does "good" really mean in practical terms for finite beings like ourselves?

If God really is infinitely greater than we are, then we should expect that it would be necessary for Him to somehow reveal to us things about Himself and His will in order for us to truly understand who He is and what He is like.

HAS THE CREATOR EVER COMMUNICATED WITH MANKIND?

The question before us, then, would be,

"Are there any records existing on this earth
that have the qualifications of actually being a
communication from the Creator to His creation about who He is, what He has done, and
what His will is for our lives?"

If such a communication existed, it would certainly seem reasonable to expect that it would be uniquely recognizable as having a divine origin. It would have to be set apart in some way from potential counterfeits so that those who were seeking to know of its existence would recognize it as such.

For example, it would be reasonable to expect that a true communication from the Creator of all things would have a specific claim to actually be from Him, and include a clear stamp of authority in some form or another. That stamp of authority would have to be something that clearly demonstrated the Creator's uniquely divine nature as all-powerful and all-knowing so that it could not be duplicated by any finite creature. True "miracles" that would be impossible for chance or a human being to accomplish would certainly fit into this category.

We would also expect this communication to exist in some kind of permanent form so that it could be passed on from one generation to another, and one culture to another, objectively and efficiently. Being in some kind of permanent form would make it far less likely to undergo corruption as it was passed along from person to person and place to place, and it would also keep the subjective biases of one group of people from unduly influencing the ability of another group to learn the truth.

Finally, it would be reasonable to expect that this

communication would date from antiquity so that it could be available to people in all times, and be widely available to people in various parts of the world.

WHAT ARE THE OPTIONS?

Very few documents actually claim to be a communication from the Creator to mankind. Of the truly ancient religious documents that have significantly influenced large populations in the world, most make no such claim.

The major religious texts in the world are the *Vedas* of Hinduism, the *Zend-Avesta* of Zoroastrianism, the *Tripitaka* of Buddhism, the *Five Classics* and *Four Books* of Confucianism, the *Qur'an* of Islam, and the Judeo-Christian Bible. Lesser known texts include the *Records of Ancient Matters* and *Chronicles of Japan* of Shinto, the *Tao Teh Ching* of Taoism, and the *Sutras* of Jainism.

Hinduism is estimated to have begun about 1500 to 1000 BC. It's a very complex religious system with no single founder, no single scripture, and no commonly agreed upon set of teachings.[33] Its writings consist primarily of prayers, chants, sacred formulas, ritualistic commentaries, and speculative philosophical treatises.

The actual date of Zoroaster (or Zarathustra) is not known, but is generally placed between 1000 and 660 BC. The *Zend-Avesta* was originally comprised of a sacred text and 21 books of commentary upon it, but only fragments remain. Zoroastrianism teaches the worship of one cosmic Power of light and goodness called Ahura Mazda, together with a coexisting cosmic Power of darkness and evil called Angra Mainyu. Neither of them is supreme in an absolute sense, although the ultimate conquest of evil by good is predicted.[34]

Shinto is the ancient religion of Japan. It consists chiefly in the worship of ancestors and nature spirits, and in a belief that there is sacred power in both animate and inanimate things. It was the state religion of Japan until 1945.[35] Shinto does not espouse a moral code, lacks religious scriptures, and does not conceive of a life after death.[36]

Taoism is one of the officially recognized religions of China. "Tao" means "way," and came to be viewed as the universal cosmic energy or impersonal being behind nature which produced the positive and negative principles of "Yin" and "Yang." Taoists believe in spiritual immortality, where the spirit of the body joins the universe after death.[37] The *Tao Teh Ching* consists of about 5,000 Chinese characters in 81 short sections in a poetic style, mainly of wise sayings and generalizations.[38]

Jainism is a nontheistic religion founded in India in the 6th century BC as a reform movement within

Hinduism. It teaches salvation by perfection through successive lives, and non-injury to living creatures.[39] Jains believe in reincarnation and seek to attain immortal bliss by escaping the continuous cycle of birth, death and rebirth. The three guiding principles of Jainism are right belief, right knowledge and right conduct.[40]

Buddhism is a religion in which the main quest of the soul is for escape from pain and suffering. Prince Siddhartha, generally referred to as Gautama Buddha, was born in India sometime around the 5th to 4th centuries BC. After leaving his wife, his newborn son and his father's inheritance, he spent several years trying to win peace through philosophic speculation and bodily asceticism. While meditating under a pipal tree, he received enlightenment. Followers of Buddhism don't acknowledge a supreme god or deity. Rather, they focus on achieving a state of inner peace and wisdom which is referred to as nirvana.[41] The *Tripitaka*, which means 3 baskets, contain rules for community living, philosophic doctrines, and the oral teachings of the Buddha.

Confucius was a philosopher and teacher who lived in ancient China from 551 to 479 BC. His thoughts on ethics, good behavior and moral virtue were written down by his disciples. Confucianism believes in ancestor worship and human-centered virtues for living a peaceful life. The writings are primarily a mixture of chronicles, magical formulas, moral laws, and songs. The golden rule of Confucianism is, "Do not do unto others what you would not want others to do unto you."[42]

None of the texts of these religions claims to be an authoritative communication from the Creator to mankind. They are held in high esteem by their followers, but neither the documents nor their original authors make the claim that they are "divinely" inspired. They are, for the most part, the philosophical speculations of thoughtful, though finite, men. None of them are widely circulated beyond their own cultural context. In fact, most people have never heard of most of them.

In contrast, the Qur'an does claim divine authority, although it does not date from truly ancient times. It is a record of revelations given to Muhammad from AD 610 to AD 632, and written down by his followers. It consists of verses grouped into 114 chapters varying in length from a few verses to 200. Much is written in rhymed Arabic prose. For hundreds of years, Muslims were hesitant to translate the Qur'an into other languages, thinking that the words of God should be preserved in their original form only. In the early 1900's, it began to be translated into Eastern and Western languages. In 1936, translations in 102 languages were known. In 2010, the number of languages had grown to 112.[43]

WHAT'S SO SPECIAL ABOUT THE BIBLE?

If the criteria we discussed earlier are acknowledged as being necessary standards for any communication to be recognized as coming from the Creator, there is really only one document in all of history that actually meets those standards. It's the one document that has been able to adapt to the needs of succeeding generations and different cultures, and has had a uniquely powerful impact on the history of the world.

The Judeo-Christian Bible claims to be the authoritative, written record of the Creator's dealings with mankind. It begins with the creation of the first man, Adam, and continues down through Abraham, who was born around 2000 BC, to Moses, who was born around 1500 BC and authored the first five books of the Hebrew Scriptures or what Christians refer to as the Old Testament. Following Moses, there is a continuing historical narrative along with prophetic and devotional writings down to Israel's King David, born around 1000 BC, through his descendants to the destruction of Jerusalem in 586 BC and its restoration under Nehemiah in 444 BC. The last book of the Old Testament was written in about 420 BC.

The New Testament begins with the birth of

Christ, and ends with the writing of the prophetic book of Revelation, dating from before the end of the first century AD.

The word "Bible" comes from a Greek term that simply means "book," and was derived from the word used for the bark of the papyrus plant used in ancient times to make paper. When talking about the Bible, however, it's important to remember that it's actually a mini-library of 66 books, rather than just one book.

The Bible was *not* written by one man ... in one place ... in one language ... in one lifetime. It was actually written over a period of about 1600 years by over 40 different authors from many different educational and cultural backgrounds. Moses was a political leader. Peter was a fisherman. Joshua was a military general. Luke was a doctor. David was a King. Matthew was a tax-collector. And Paul was a rabbi and tentmaker.

It was written on three continents – Europe, Asia, and Africa. In three languages – Hebrew, Aramaic and Greek. In many different places. Moses wrote while in the wilderness. Paul wrote while in prison. And Daniel wrote in a palace. It was written by men in different moods, from the heights of joy to the depths of despair. It deals with many controversial subjects, ranging from discussions about the nature of God, the nature of sin, the existence of life after death and

God's will for mankind to ethical questions relating to telling the truth, appropriate roles and lifestyles, abortion, capital punishment, poverty and justice, and a host of other dilemmas facing man and his relationships with others.

Throughout the entire series of books, however, there is a consistency in its message and harmony in its teachings. To put that into context, think of how difficult it would be to get a consistent message from a collection of religious works from AD 400 to the present. The God of the Qur'an (AD 600s) is impersonal, is known only from natural signs and can only be spoken about in parables.[44] The God of the Book of Mormon (early 1800's) has a perfected, glorified, physical body like a man,[45] and has a harem from which are produced spirit children who indwell the bodies of material children born on this earth.[46] The God of Neitzche (late 1800s) is dead!

HOW WIDELY AVAILABLE IS IT?

The Bible was the first major book printed on Gutenberg's press. Since then, it has been translated into every major language in the world, plus hundreds of other languages spoken only by relatively small groups of tribal peoples living in remote areas of the world. Most of these people had no written language until Bible translators went to live with them, learn their language, commit it to writing, and then translate the Bible. For many of them, the Bible is the first and only document in print.

To help understand how widely translated the Bible is, consider the fact that the world's largest library catalog lists almost 500 million bibliographic records in a total of 483 languages.[47] By contrast, Wycliffe Bible Translators notes that the complete Bible has been translated into 704 languages, the complete New Testament into 1,551 languages, and at least some portion of the Bible has been translated into an additional 1,160 languages – bringing the total number of languages having at least some part of the Bible to 3,415, with more languages being added each year.[48]

Not only is the Bible the most widely translated document in the world, it is also, without question, the most widely distributed document in the world. More copies of the Bible have been sold or given away than any other book in all of history. In fact, no other book even begins to compare with the Bible when it comes to the number of copies in circulation. Every year, the Bible is the world's number one best-selling book.

Discovering exactly how many copies of the Bible have been distributed is impossible because Bibles have been produced by so many different and unrelated publishers, and many Bibles are given away rather than sold. However, one survey estimated the total distribution for all Bibles worldwide up to the year 1992 at 6 billion.[49]

Most people know that almost every hotel room in America has a copy of the Bible placed there by The Gideons International. As of 2021, that organization alone has placed or distributed more than 2 billion Bibles and New Testaments worldwide since its founding in 1908.[50] Members currently distribute more than 80 million Bibles annually.[51]

To put those numbers in perspective – the number 1 best-selling book of all time outside of the Bible is *Don Quixote* by Miguel de Cervantes. Since its publication in two parts in 1605 and 1615, it has sold approximately 500 million copies. *A Tale of Two Cities* by Charles Dickens ranks second at about 200 million copies. *The Lord of the Rings* by J.R.R. Tolkien ranks third at about 150 million copies, with *Harry Potter and the Sorcerer's Stone* next at approximately 107 million.[52]

WHAT'S BEEN ITS IMPACT?

The Bible has withstood the pressures of time, persecution and criticism, and is studied diligently by millions of people today. None of the other sacred writings of the world has been subjected to anywhere near the scrutiny and criticism that the Bible has undergone, nor has any other literature been given the praise that has been accorded the Bible. The influence of the Bible on literature, music, and the arts is absolutely unmatched by any other book.

In fact, the impact of this book has been so significant that the world measures time in relation to when its major character, Jesus of Nazareth, was born. Every significant, and insignificant, person or event occurring before Jesus was born we identify as BC – Before Christ. And, every significant, and insignificant, person or event occurring after His birth we identify as AD – *Anno Domini*, which is Latin for, "In the year of our Lord." Even the scheme used by Middle Eastern archeologists of BCE and CE acknowledge that the "Common Era" began with the birth of Christ.

The dictionary definition of the word "unique" is, "having no like or equal; unparalleled; incomparable."[53]

When compared with the other works of religious literature in the world, the Bible fits that definition as no other book in all of history.

4

IS THE BIBLE 'GOD'S WORD'?

*"If you cross the river, a great
empire will be destroyed."*

Those prophetic words were given to Croesus, the king of Lydia, when he asked the Oracle at Delphi if he should attack Cyrus the Great of Persia. Delighted with the prophecy, he saw it as a clear sign of victory and went ahead with the invasion. After all, with this confirmation coming straight from the most respected oracle in the ancient world, he was sure to win.

It was common at that time in history for armies to disband during winter and Croesus did so, expecting his adversary to do the same. Cyrus, however, did not. Instead, he attacked and defeated Croesus, and later captured him.[54] Croesus clearly saw the fulfillment of the prophecy given to him by the Delphic Oracle. Unfortunately, the great empire that was destroyed was his own!

The Oracle at Delphi was one of the most sought after places in the ancient world for seeking knowledge of what would happen in the future. According to Cicero of Rome, its influence was so significant that no one undertook an expedition or sent out a colony, and no distinguished individual of the Empire conducted business without the sanction of the oracle.[55]

It was believed that the oracle was located where a huge serpent named Python had been slain by the infant god Apollo. Its body then fell into a deep crevice, and the fumes from its decaying carcass gave off vapors that put a priestess, called the Pythia, into a trance where she would be filled with the divine presence of Apollo.[56] The oracles were delivered in a frenzied state induced by the fumes, and priests would interpret the sometimes incomprehensible words and turn them into prophetic utterances given to those who came for advice.[57]

According to the ancient historian, Diodorus, the Pythia was initially a young virgin whose chastity and purity was reserved for union with the god. However, in the late 3rd century BC Echecrates of Thessaly was enamored with the young and beautiful woman, kidnapped her and then raped her. Because of this deplorable act, the leaders of Delphi passed a law that all future Pythias be women over fifty years old who dressed and wore jewelry to resemble a young virgin.

Like the oracle given to Croesus, the guidance given by the Pythia or the priests who interpreted what she said was generally in the form of cryptic messages or educated guesses phrased in such a way that the oracle would always be right.

On one occasion, Alexander the Great visited the Delphi Oracle and wanted an answer regarding whether he would soon conquer the ancient world. The Pythia refused to give him a direct answer and asked him to come back later. Alexander then grabbed her by the hair and dragged her out of the chamber. To which she cried, "You are invincible, my son!"

Alexander dropped her, saying, "Now I have my answer!"[58]

THUS SAYS THE LORD!

It's one thing to *say* that a prophetic message is from a god or God, and quite another to prove that it actually is! So, what about the Bible? In contrast to most religious literature, the Bible actually claims to be the uniquely authoritative communication to mankind from the Creator of all things.

The phrase, *thus says the LORD* or its equivalent, occurs over 2,500 times in the Bible.

In His Sermon on the Mount, Jesus specifically said,

"I tell you the truth, until heaven and earth disappear, not the smallest letter, not the least stroke of a pen, will by any means disappear from the Law until everything is accomplished."[59]

The apostle Peter wrote,

"Above all, you must understand that no prophecy of Scripture came about by the prophet's own interpretation. For prophecy never had its origin in the will of man, but men spoke from God as they were carried along by the Holy Spirit."[60]

St. Paul wrote in his letter to Timothy,

"All Scripture is God-breathed and is useful for teaching, rebuking, correcting and training in righteousness, so that the man of God may be thoroughly equipped for every good work."[61]

HAS THE BIBLE FORETOLD THE FUTURE?

Unlike the Oracle at Delphi or other religious literature, the predictive prophecy in the Bible is very specific.

If the Creator alone knows all things, then only He would be able to foretell the future with certainty.

To accurately predict specific details of future events would be a wonderful stamp of authority to show that a specific document is the work of a supernatural Creator, and that all other claimants are liars. And that is actually the approach the Bible takes:

> "'Present your case,' says the LORD. 'Set forth
> your arguments,' says Jacob's King. 'Bring in
> your idols to tell us what is going to happen.
> Tell us what the former things were, so that
> we may consider them and know their final
> outcome. Or declare to us the things to come,
> tell us what the future holds, so we may know
> that you are gods...
>
> "I am the LORD; that is my name! I will not give
> my glory to another or my praise to idols. See,
> the former things have taken place, and new
> things I declare; before they spring into being I
> announce them to you.'"[62]

In the Bible, people are named before birth, kingdoms are outlined before their historical existence, and battles are described before they occurred. Predictive prophecy is one of most important distinctive features of the Bible, and it's not found in any other of the world's religions.

"No well accredited prophecy is found in any

other book or even oral tradition now extant, or that has ever been extant in the world. The oracles of heathenism are not to be classed as exceptions. There is not a single one of them that meets the tests required to prove supernatural agency, which every Scripture prophecy evinces. So far as we have been able to find, there is no exception to this sweeping remark."[63]

The gods of paganism are limited in their powers and do not claim absolute knowledge. The myriad of gods each supposedly holds a certain degree of power or influence in a very limited sphere – whether it be a god of fire or water or wind or love or hate or whatever. But none claims to be the absolute Creator and sovereign Lord of all things, and their worshipers acknowledge their limitations.

In many ways, pagan gods are like the mascots of sports teams today. The Wolverines or Wildcats or Nittany Lions or Spartans or Trojans or Seminoles all have powerful characteristics that their followers lift up and revere. They also have traditional activities and rituals whereby their followers seek to transfer to themselves the unique powers that these "deities" represent.

But none is considered in any way absolute. None

of the pagan gods can assure the future outcome of an engagement with another foe ... just like none of those sports teams can guarantee a win.

HOW ARE TRUE PROPHETS TESTED?

The Bible sets forth two tests that any prophet must meet in order to be considered a true spokesman for the LORD.

The first test is that 100% of what a true prophet predicts must come true. If the prophet is only 99% correct, he is a false prophet.

That's a pretty tough standard! However, if the Creator of all things knows the future with certainty, and if a prophet is truly proclaiming what this Creator has told him to proclaim, then there is really no question that what the prophet says must certainly come to pass.

"You may say to yourselves, 'How can we know when a message has not been spoken by the LORD?' If what a prophet proclaims in the name of the LORD does *not* take place or come true, that is a message the LORD has *not* spoken. That prophet has spoken presumptuously. Do not be afraid of him."[64]

The second Biblical test of a prophet focuses on the unchanging character of God's nature. Because God doesn't change with time, whatever a true prophet says today must be consistent with what has been revealed through true prophets in the past. This is vitally important because at times, whether it results from an educated guess or a chance occurrence, some things that false prophets predict are bound to come true.

> "If a prophet, or one who foretells by dreams,
> appears among you and announces to you a
> miraculous sign or wonder, and if the sign or
> wonder of which he has spoken takes place,
> and he says, 'Let us follow other gods (gods
> you have not known) and let us worship
> them,' you must not listen to the words of
> that prophet or dreamer ... That prophet or
> dreamer must be put to death, because he has
> preached rebellion against the LORD your
> God..."[65]

The predictions of true prophets are always correct, and they are always consistent with what has been proclaimed by true prophets in the past.

CYRUS AND JERUSALEM

Two of the most amazing prophecies in the Bible relate directly to Cyrus the Great, the Persian emperor who not only defeated Croesus but who is the only non-Jewish person in the Bible who God refers to as His "anointed."

Cyrus (c. 600-530 BC) was a brilliant military strategist and administrator who, unlike other authoritarian rulers in antiquity and even today, respected the customs and religions of the lands he conquered. The Greek historian Xenophon described Cyrus' heroism in battle and his abilities and practices as a king and legislator in his book, *Cyropaedia*, which influenced Thomas Jefferson and his drafting of the US Declaration of Independence. Cyrus created the largest empire the ancient world had ever seen, and which may be to this day the largest empire ever.[66] He was the first world leader to be called "the Great."

Interestingly, compared to the massive structures that other ancient leaders built for their final resting places, the tomb of Cyrus is noteworthy for its extreme modesty and simplicity with a simple inscription that was equally modest.

> "O man, whosoever thou art, and from whencesoever thou comest (for I know thou wilt come), I am Cyrus, the founder of the Persian Empire; do not grudge me this little earth which covers my body."

The prophet Isaiah wrote between 740 and 681 BC, long before the birth of Cyrus, in part to demonstrate to his own and future generations that the LORD is the only true God. He alone is able to foretell the future, and He challenges other "gods" to do the same.

Earlier in his book, Isaiah had prophesied that Jerusalem would be destroyed and many of its citizens taken captive. Now, he tells the people that the city will again be rebuilt and inhabited, and he specifically names the man who will be responsible for allowing the Jews to return to their land. His name will be Cyrus. He tells his readers that the reason he is being so specific is so that they will know that the LORD really is the only true God.

"This is what the Lord says – your Redeemer,
who formed you in the womb:

"I am the LORD, who has made all things,
who alone stretched out the heavens, who
spread out the earth by Myself, who foils the
signs of false prophets, and makes fools of
diviners, who overthrows the learning of the
wise and turns it into nonsense, who carries
out the words of His servants and fulfills the
predictions of His messengers, who says of
Jerusalem, 'It shall be inhabited,' of the towns
of Judah, 'They shall be built,' and of their
ruins, 'I will restore them,' who says to the
watery deep, 'Be dry, and I will dry up your

streams,' who says of Cyrus, 'He is my shepherd and will accomplish all that I please; he will say of Jerusalem, 'Let it be rebuilt,' and of the temple, 'Let its foundations be laid.'

"... I will give you the treasures of darkness, riches stored in secret places, so that you may know that I am the LORD, the God of Israel, who summons you by name."[67]

In fulfillment of Isaiah's prophecy, Jerusalem was completely destroyed by Nebuchadnezzar of Babylon in 586 BC and its inhabitants were taken into exile. In 539 BC, over a century and a half after Isaiah wrote his prophecy, Cyrus the Great, leader of the Medo-Persian Empire defeated Babylon and later issued a decree allowing the exiled Jews to return to their homeland. And not only did he allow the captives from Israel to return, he even made provision for rebuilding the city – a city that has had a very long and varied history and remains the center of world political interest even in our day.

The decree of Cyrus was recorded by Ezra the scribe.

"This is what Cyrus king of Persia says: 'The LORD, the God of heaven, has given me all the kingdoms of the earth and he has appointed me to build a temple for him at Jerusalem in Judah. Anyone of his people among you – may his God be with him, and let him go up to Jerusalem in Judah and build the temple of the LORD, the God of Israel, the God who is in Jerusalem. And the people of any place where survivors may now be living are to provide him with silver and gold, with goods and livestock, and with freewill offerings for the temple of God in Jerusalem.'"[68]

There is corroborating evidence of the practice of Cyrus to allow captive nations to return to their homelands from an extra-Biblical source. In 1879, a clay cylinder inscribed with Babylonian cuneiform markings was found with an account by Cyrus, king of Persia, of his conquest of Babylon in 539 BC. Cyrus claimed to have accomplished this great feat with the help of Marduk, the god of Babylon.

It had been the practice of the Babylonian kings to destroy the sanctuaries of the gods of the nations they defeated. They then deported the people of those nations to other parts of their empire in order to prevent them from uniting together and rising up in revolt. Cyrus, however, did not follow this practice.

In light of the fact that the god of the Babylonians did not support their king when he attacked, Cyrus did not assume that his gods would always support him in his military efforts. He sought to marshal the strength of any and every god that people worshipped in order to have them all on his side. He returned the images of the various gods to their people. He provided for the restoration of their destroyed sanctuaries. And, he allowed the people to return to their homelands with the request that they pray for his well-being every day.

The actual inscription on what is referred to as the Cyrus Cylinder reads as follows:

"From [Shuanna] I sent back to their places
... the gods who lived therein, and made
permanent sanctuaries for them. I collected
together all of their people and returned them
to their settlements, and the gods of the land
... I returned them unharmed to their cells, in
the sanctuaries that make them happy. May
all the gods that I returned to their sanctuaries,
every day before Bel and Nabu, ask for a long
life for me, and mention my good deeds..."[69]

Although the Jews are not mentioned in this document, their return to Palestine following their deportation by Nebuchadnezzar was part of this policy. Since they had no images of God, they took with them the sacred vessels from the Temple.

The fulfillment of Isaiah's prophecies concerning Cyrus and Jerusalem came about over 150 years after Isaiah's death.

CYRUS AND BABYLON

Cyrus was not only the agent God used to restore and rebuild Jerusalem, he was also God's agent in fulfilling another of Isaiah's prophecies concerning the defeat of the capital city of the most powerful empire of its day.

The city of Babylon, located about 54 miles south of modern Baghdad, is considered by many to be the greatest city in antiquity. It occupied a very strategic location on the Euphrates River that enabled it to carry on trade with all the regions of the known world. It was a center of culture and learning, with its Hanging Gardens considered one of the seven wonders of the ancient world. Its defenses were an engineering marvel, and if correct according to ancient historians, would have successfully withstood siege by an army at any time in history up until the development of aircraft and the sophisticated artillery of World War II.

The Greek historian Herodotus tells us that Babylon was a huge city with a 56 mile circumference covering an area of 196 square miles. It was completely surrounded by double walls and a 30 foot wide moat with 100 gates of solid brass. The outer wall was about 335 feet high, 85 feet thick, and extended about 35 feet below the ground. It had 250 watchtowers that rose to a height of about 400 feet. The spaces between the towers were wide enough for a 4 horse chariot to turn around.[70] To put those dimensions into perspective – the outer wall surrounding the city was about as tall as a 30 story building, and wide enough to fit 11 cars abreast. The towers were as high as a 40 story building!

Herodotus may have been exaggerating on the dimensions. Another ancient historian, Ctesias, says the walls were 300 feet high, with the circumference of the city 42 miles.[71] Strabo tells us that the walls were 35 feet thick.[72] One thing is very clear from all accounts, however. The ancient city of Babylon was astounding in its size, splendor, and the strength of its fortifications.

The Biblical prophet Jeremiah alluded to the massive fortifications when he said,

"'Even if Babylon reaches to the sky and fortifies her lofty stronghold, I will send destroyers against her,' declares the LORD."[73]

A unique feature of the city was the fact that the Euphrates River flowed under its walls, providing a plentiful supply of drinking water for the entire population, along with plenty of water for cultivating crops in the event of a long siege. To assure that it could not be reduced by famine, an extensive space between the inner and outer walls provided plenty of room for raising grain and fodder for the city while also providing space to shelter the population of the surrounding villages during an invasion. The city's leadership and people were rightfully confident that no army would ever be able to successfully storm the city.

However, in contrast to the Biblical predictions that the destroyed city of Jerusalem would one day be rebuilt and restored, the prophetic message about the impregnable city of Babylon was that it would be defeated and become a desolate waste.

Over 150 years before Cyrus approached Babylon, the prophet Isaiah wrote:

> "See, I will stir up against them the Medes, who do not care for silver and have no delight in gold. Their bows will strike down the young men; they will have no mercy on infants nor will they look with compassion on children.

> "Babylon, the Jewel of kingdoms, the glory of the Babylonians' pride, will be overthrown by God like Sodom and Gomorrah. She will never be inhabited or lived in through all generations; no Arab will pitch his tent there, no

shepherd will rest his flocks there. But desert creatures will lie there, jackals will fill her houses; there the owls will dwell, and there the wild goats will leap about. Hyenas will howl in her strongholds, jackals in her luxurious palaces. Her time is at hand, and her days will not be prolonged."[74]

Isaiah predicted that the Medes would be the people God would use to defeat Babylon, that the city would be completely overthrown and never be inhabited or lived in through all generations, that no Arab would pitch his tent or shepherd his flocks there, and that desert creatures and wild animals would occupy its strongholds.

So completely was this prophecy fulfilled that, until Claudius James Rich conducted his archeological excavation of Babylon in 1811-1812 and again in 1817, the knowledge that Babylon even existed was based solely on the written accounts of the Old Testament and a few Greek writers.[75]

Cyrus the Great, the leader of the Mede and Persian forces, approached the city of Babylon in 539 BC to lay siege against it. After recognizing the futility of any attempt to successfully storm its walls, he looked for another way to enter it.

According to the Herodotus, Cyrus ordered his

troops to dig huge canals to divert the water of the Euphrates river away from its normal path under the walls of the city.[76] He then made plans to march under the walls and attack the city from within while the Babylonians were carousing at an annual feast to their gods. The account of what happened inside the city that night is recorded by a later Biblical prophet, Daniel, and the secular historian Xenophon.[77]

Belshazzar, who was co-regent with his father Nabonidus, held a great feast for a thousand of his nobles and drank wine with them. While he was drinking the wine, he gave orders to bring in the gold and silver goblets that had been taken by his grandfather Nebuchadnezzar from the Temple in Jerusalem. As he praised the gods of gold, silver, bronze, iron, wood and stone, Belshazzar literally saw the handwriting on the wall!

The fingers of a human hand suddenly appeared and wrote on the plaster of the wall inside the royal palace.

"Numbered ... Numbered ... Weighed ...
Divided!"

Daniel interpreted the inscription for the king:

"God has *numbered* the days of your reign and brought it to an end. You have been *weighed*

on the scales and found wanting. Your kingdom is *divided* and given to the Medes and
Persians."[78]

The city was captured on October 13, 539 BC. From
that time on, it began to decay. One of Cyrus' succes-
sors, Xerxes, plundered it. 200 years after its defeat,
Alexander the Great wanted to restore the city's great
temple of Marduk, but was deterred by the prohibitive
cost. After Alexander's death, Babylon was the focus
of political struggles and battles for control among his
generals. The net result was more plundering. When
it finally came under the control of the Seleucids, it
was so badly shattered that it soon became apparent
that rebuilding the once magnificent city would be
more costly than building a new city. A new city was
constructed on a site 40 miles north of Babylon on the
Tigris River, and Babylon was eventually completely
abandoned.

For centuries, not even Bedouins traveled there.
The character of the soil prevented the growth of veg-
etation suitable for the pasturage of flocks, and various superstitions among the Arabs kept them from
pitching their tents in that region. It was occupied by
desert creatures and wild animals.

Jerusalem, Athens, Rome and other great ancient
cities remain today. But, Babylon, the most magnifi-

cent of them all, is a desolate wasteland in exact accordance with what the Bible said would happen.

THE CITY OF TYRE

The ancient seacoast city of Tyre was the subject of a prophecy recorded in Ezekiel chapter 26.[79]

> "... this is what the sovereign LORD says: I am against you, O Tyre, and I will bring many nations against you, like the sea casting up its waves. They will destroy the walls of Tyre and pull down her towers; I will scrape away her rubble and make her a bare rock.

> "... They will plunder your wealth and loot your merchandise; they will break down your walls and demolish your fine houses and throw your stones, timber and rubble into the sea. I will put an end to your noisy songs, and the music of your harps will be heard no more. I will make you a bare rock, and you will become a place to spread fishnets. You will never be rebuilt, for I the LORD have spoken, declares the Sovereign LORD."[80]

Ezekiel wrote around 590 BC when Tyre was a powerful city/state on the coast of the Mediterranean Sea. Because they rejoiced at the destruction of Jerusalem, the prophet predicted that they, too, would one day be destroyed. There is nothing particularly profound about that, since cities and nations have risen and fallen throughout history. It's the specific details of how that destruction would take place that make this prophecy so remarkable.

Ezekiel explained that God would bring many nations against Tyre, "like the sea casting up its waves." He went on to say that God will "scrape away her rubble and make her a bare rock." The stones, timber and rubble from her destruction will be thrown into the sea, and this once powerful city/state will never be rebuilt.

The ancient city of Tyre was actually a two-part city – Old Tyre on the mainland, and an island fortress about ½ mile off the coast. The first wave of the attacks against Tyre came when Nebuchadnezzar of Babylon laid siege against the city in 585 BC, and finally defeated it in 573 BC. That could easily have been a lucky guess by Ezekiel, since Babylon was the major power in that part of the world at the time. Nebuchadnezzar broke down the gates and entered the mainland city, only to find that most of the inhabitants had moved themselves and their wealth by ship to the island fortress.

The next "wave" takes the prophecy out of the realm of lucky guesses and places it clearly in the realm of the amazing.

About 240 years later, in 333 BC, Alexander the Great marched through this part of the world conquering everything in his path. He desired to sacrifice in the temple of Heracles on the island city of Tyre, but the citizens of Tyre refused. They felt secure in their island fortress, and did not acquiesce to Alexander's demands. Instead, they killed Alexander's ambassadors and threw their bodies from the top of the walls into the sea. This act angered Alexander and embittered his troops.

Up until that time, no one had been able to take the island fortress because Tyre had the only navy capable of doing it. Not to be deterred, Alexander did what no one else had thought of doing. He ordered his men to demolish the ruins of the old city and throw the debris into the water to build a ½ mile, 200 foot wide land bridge across the span of water separating the old city from the fortress. The debris from the city was not sufficient to span the distance, so Alexander commanded his men to literally scrape up the dirt with their shields until they reached underlying rock, and use the dirt to help finish the land bridge.

The task was completed in about six months – from January to June 332 BC – after which Alexander brought in his siege equipment and took the city with the aid of ships from Persia and Cyprus. The walls of the fortress were destroyed. Six thousand of the fighting men were killed within the city and two thousand crucified on the beach. About 30,000 of Tyre's inhabitants were sold into slavery. Alexander lost about 400 men.

The city was rebuilt and besieged several times after its destruction by Alexander. In AD 638, Arabs conquered the city. In 1124, it was taken by the Crusaders. And, in 1291, the Mameluke Muslims took it and reduced the city to ashes. Their policy was to make the destruction so severe that the Crusaders would not be tempted to ever reoccupy it. Tyre's citizens were killed, dispersed or sold into slavery, and their houses, temples, buildings and monuments burned.

The rubble from the mainland city of Tyre was so thoroughly cleaned out by Alexander's troops that its precise location today is a point of controversy. Ships during the 1800's usually bypassed the area, except to occasionally stop and gloat over it. Visitors at the time reported seeing only a tiny fishing village on the mainland, with fishermen drying their nets on the bare rock.

The country of Lebanon has been developing the modern city of Tyre as a tourist attraction in recent years. However, remains of the great structures of Ezekiel's day, including the palace and temple of Heracles, have never been found. They lie hidden under water or under the ruins of later Hellenistic and Roman structures. The city that was once an arrogant and prosperous commercial superpower was completely destroyed.

WHAT ABOUT ALL THOSE ERRORS AND CONTRADICTIONS?

A central mark of Christianity as opposed to other religions and philosophies is that Christianity can be verified historically. The *subjective* truth that it claims to teach is grounded in *objective* truth.

I have often talked with people about the uniqueness of the Bible and received the response, "Yeah, but what about all those errors and contradictions?" I usually respond by asking them to name one so I can answer it specifically. Invariably, the response then is, "Well, I don't really know where they are, but I know they're there!"

In truth, the Bible is *not* full of errors and contradictions. In fact, over and over again, statements that were at one time considered to be errors or contradictions have, upon more mature reflection or as the result of some archaeological discovery, been proven to be precisely accurate. In often extraordinary ways, modern archaeology has confirmed the truth of what the Bible says, many times in direct opposition to what critics have expounded.

For example, 19th Century Biblical critic, Julius

Wellhausen, confidently asserted that the first five books of the Bible could not possibly have been written by Moses because writing had not been invented, or at least was not in common use, until centuries after Moses' death. Thus the first five books of the Bible must have been the product of oral tradition written down at a much later time.[81] Archaeologists have since discovered thousands of stone tablets and monuments that have provided abundant proof that many written languages were in common use long before the time of Moses.

Biblical skeptics often pointed to the fact that no record of a Hittite nation had ever been found in extra-Biblical literature. They concluded that the Hittites were therefore a myth created by the Biblical writers. Then, in 1887, excavations at Amarna in Egypt uncovered the diplomatic correspondence between Pharaoh Amenhotep III and his son, Akhenaten, which contained letters with the Hittites. Later, starting in 1906, a royal archive with 10,000 tablets were discovered near Carchemish and Boghazkoi, and the ruins of their capital city of Khorsabad were excavated, telling of the Hittites as a very powerful people in that region of the world.[82]

In 1925, more than 1,000 clay tablets were found in Nuzi, Iraq shedding light on life in Biblical times. Prior to that time, skeptics had said that the account of Esau selling his birthright to his brother, Jacob, was clearly a made up story unfounded historically. The tablets confirmed the historical basis of the Jacob and Esau transaction with the account of Tupkitilla who sold his birthright to his brother Kurpazah for 3 sheep. They also confirmed the practice of a barren wife making a slave her surrogate, as happened with Sarah and Hagar.[83]

Genesis 14 mentions four kings who formed a coalition to fight against five kings in battles in the area around the Dead Sea. Critics rejected this, too, as a myth saying the names of the kings were fictional and that there was no extensive travel like what was mentioned in the Bible at that time in history. Then, in 1933, the Mari tablets were found with the names of two of the kings mentioned in Genesis 14, along with the mention of practices that are similar to those mentioned by Abraham, Isaac and Jacob.[84]

Genesis 37:28 mentions that Joseph was sold by his brothers into slavery for 20 shekels of silver. That price matches precisely the going price of slaves in the 19th and 18th centuries BC as affirmed by other ancient documents from that region.[85] Interestingly, the price of slaves in the 8th century BC had risen to 50 or 60 shekels, and in the 5th and 4th centuries BC to between 90 and 120 shekels.

Because no record of David's existence had ever

been found in ancient documents outside the Bible, skeptics had long argued that David was a mere legend, invented by Hebrew scribes to dignify Israel's past. Then, in 1993, an inscription was found on a stone monument in Tel-Dan from the 9th century BC commemorating a military victory by the king of Damascus over two of his foes. One was the "king of Israel." The other was the "House of David."[86]

Skeptical scholars had often suggested that the Philistines, who are mentioned in many encounters with the ancient Israelites before, during, and after the time of David were also invented by priestly scribes who wanted to dramatize how powerful David's mythical dynasty was. Modern archaeology has now uncovered a wealth of information about the Philistines that is thoroughly consistent with the Biblical narratives. Numerous Egyptian inscriptions mention them, and material has been found that shows that the Philistines were expert metalworkers, in accordance with what is said about them in the Bible.[87]

At one time the existence of the cities of Nineveh and Babylon, and the existence of a king named Belshazzar in Babylon were considered highly questionable, until archaeological discoveries were made that confirmed the Biblical data in each case to be true. Belshazzar was actually the co-regent with his absent father, Nabonidus. Thus, when the Bible recorded that Belshazzar offered Daniel the position of "third highest ruler in the kingdom" when he saw the handwriting on the wall, it was exactly right![88]

Jesus of Nazareth lived only about 33 years in a remote section of the Roman Empire. His public ministry lasted only about 3 ½ years. Yet, archaeologists have discovered much about the life and times of Jesus that supports and illuminates what is reported by the Biblical writers.

In 1961, archaeologists were excavating the ruins of Caesarea Maritima, the ancient seat of Roman government in Judea. They uncovered a first-century inscription identifying the Roman governor at the time of Jesus' crucifixion who had dedicated a temple to the people of Caesarea in honor of the emperor. The inscription read, "The prefect of Judaea, Pontius Pilate, erected the Tiberium (in honor of Tiberius Caesar)."[89]

In 1968 the skeletal remains of a crucified man were found in a burial cave at Giva'at ha-Mitvar outside Jerusalem. This was the first time that the actual remains of a crucified victim had ever been found. The remains dramatically corroborated the Bible's description of the Roman method of crucifixion. The open arms had been nailed to a crossbar, the knees had been doubled up and turned sideways with a single large iron nail driven through both heels. The shin bones seemed to have been broken, and the body had been placed in a family grave.[90]

In 1990, workers building a water park 2 miles south of the Temple Mount in Jerusalem accidentally broke through the ceiling of a hidden burial chamber dating to the first century AD. Inside, archaeologists found an ossuary containing the bones of a 60 year old man with the inscription, "Joseph, son of Caiaphas." Experts believe these are the actual bones of Caiaphas, the high priest who ordered the arrest of Jesus and turned him over to the Romans to be crucified.[91]

It can be safely stated that no archaeological discovery has ever disproved what the Bible has said. Rather, the numerous discoveries made by archaeologists over the years have always confirmed that what is said in the Bible as it relates to historical events is true.

Is the Bible God's Word? It definitely claims to be so. It has correctly reported details about events in the distant past and accurately foretold many specific things about future events, including predictions about the coming Messiah that were literally fulfilled in Jesus of Nazareth.

5

IS JESUS OF NAZARETH THE MESSIAH?

"Jesus is a disappointment ... and a threat!"

That was the sentiment of the Jewish leaders in Jerusalem when an itinerant preacher suddenly appeared on the scene claiming to be Israel's long-awaited Messiah – the One sent by God to deliver His people from bondage. *Messiah* is the Hebrew word for "Anointed One," and *Christ* is the translation of the word into the Greek of the New Testament. Jesus would later be executed as a criminal.

When His followers began saying that He had risen from the dead, these leaders were furious. They arrested two of His disciples, Peter and John, and wanted to put them to death. But a wise member of their council, a man named Gamaliel, stepped in to offer a word of caution.[92]

"If this is just another movement arising from human enthusiasm it will die out soon enough.

But then again, if God is in this, you won't be able to stop it — unless, of course, you're ready to fight against God!"

Gamaliel reminded them of two other men in the recent past who led revolts against the Romans. They were killed and their followers quickly dispersed. If Jesus was just a man like them, this movement would also fail. If it didn't, they needed to be careful! The other Jewish leaders couldn't really argue with what he said, so they let Peter and John go after having them flogged and ordering them not to speak again in the name of Jesus.

One of the major problems was that Jesus didn't fit the profile of what these leaders wanted their Messiah to be. They were looking for a military leader who would deliver them from bondage to their Roman overlords, not a spiritual leader who would bring deliverance on earth from bondage to sin and death. But in AD 132, about a century after Gamaliel gave his advice, the Jewish leaders in Jerusalem found what they were looking for.

The Roman emperor Hadrian established a colony in Jerusalem in an attempt to integrate the Jews into the empire. He banned the practice of circumcision and built a temple to the Roman god Jupiter over the ruins of the Jewish Temple.[93] That infuriated the Jews.

As a result, a military leader named Simon bar Kosba arose and led what was initially a very successful revolt against Rome. He badly defeated the Romans' Egyptian Legion XXII and established an independent government over most of the Judean province that lasted for about 3 years, declaring himself to be the Head of State.

The greatest rabbi of the time, Akiva ben Yosef, hailed him as the long-awaited Messiah and gave him a new name – bar Kokhba – which was a messianic reference meaning "Son of the Star."

He was nothing like Jesus of Nazareth. The Talmud says that his army consisted of about 200,000 men who he compelled to prove their loyalty by each man cutting off one of his fingers. Whenever he would go into battle, he was reported as praying, "O Master of the universe, there is no need for you to assist us against our enemies, but do not embarrass us either."[94]

When the Romans realized what was happening in a remote part of the empire, the emperor Hadrian came from Rome to personally oversee the war effort. With the aid of the men of Legion X, he retook Jerusalem and killed bar Kokhba, along with a recorded 580,000 Jewish casualties. The remnant of the Jewish population was exiled and Jerusalem was subsequently barred to Jews.

In line with what Gamaliel said about movements

arising from human origins, the military uprising the Jewish leaders were looking for failed when its leader was killed. Bar Kokhba's name had initially been changed to indicate that he was the Deliverer the Jews had been waiting for. After his defeat and death, his name was changed again. This time to bar Koziba – meaning, "son of the lie."[95]

So, what about Jesus? Was He really the Messiah who God had promised would deliver His people from bondage in fulfillment of many Old Testament prophecies, or was He just another failed claimant like bar Kokhba?

IDENTIFYING THE MESSIAH

In order to identify any one person out of all the billions of people who have ever lived, are living, or will ever live, you don't need a *lot* of information. What you need is *specific* information. If you knew the family line someone is from, their time in history and where that person was born, you would be able to identify anyone. In addition, some unique characteristic of the person would enable you to confirm that a specific individual is the one you are looking for.

For example, I am the only person in the history of the world who is the firstborn son in the family line of William Sarris, born in a small town in upstate New York after the end of World War II but before the beginning of the new millennium in the year 2000, who wrote a book published in 2023 titled, *Searching for Truth in Vegas, Hollywood & Bethlehem*. No one else who has ever lived or will ever live fits that description.

THE COMING MESSIAH ... WHO?

The first prediction in the Bible of the future Messiah comes in the third chapter of the first book, Genesis, which covers the events of creation down through the time of Joseph who died about 1615 BC. It was written by Moses around 1450 BC.

After Adam and Eve disobeyed God by eating from the tree He had specifically told them not to eat from, God explained that He would one day raise up a descendant of the woman who would deliver mankind from the effects of sin and death. God said to the Serpent who deceived Eve,

> "I will put enmity between you and the woman,
>   and between your offspring and hers; he
>   will crush your head, and you will strike his
>   heel."[96]

That's not a particularly specific prophecy. The one who would ultimately defeat the Serpent and be wounded in the process would be a human being who would be the offspring of the woman. That could fit just about anyone who has ever lived. The only slightly unusual thing about it is the reference to the future Deliverer as the offspring of the *woman*. In the Jewish culture at the time when this was written, that would have been somewhat surprising. Property rights, tribal and royal lineages, and genealogical records were determined on the basis of the descendants of the man, not the woman.

After that general prophetic word, God began to limit who that Deliverer would be by calling Abram, who would later be named Abraham, from among all the people who then lived and telling him that it would be through his family line that all the nations of the world would be blessed.[97]

Abraham had two sons, Ishmael and Isaac. It would have been natural to assume that the promise originally given to Eve and then to Abraham would be fulfilled through a descendant of the elder son, Ishmael. But God further narrowed who the Messiah would be by saying that He would descend from the second son, Isaac.[98] Isaac also had two sons – Esau and Jacob – but it was again the younger son, Jacob, who was chosen to be the ancestor of the future Deliverer.[99]

God further narrowed down who the "offspring of the woman" would be when Jacob blessed his twelve sons at the end of his life. The promise would not be fulfilled through the family line of his firstborn son, Reuben, nor through Jacob's favorite son, Joseph. The future Deliverer would come through the line of Judah, whose descendants would become the ruling family in Israel.[100]

Hundreds of years passed until about 1050 BC when Israel chose a king. Their first king was Saul from the tribe of Benjamin, but he disobeyed the God of his fathers. He was followed by David who, in fulfillment of the prophetic word through Jacob, was from the tribe of Judah. God specifically promised David that one of his direct descendants would rule on an everlasting throne.

> "When your days are over and you rest with
> your fathers, I will raise up your offspring to
> succeed you, who will come from your own
> body, and I will establish his kingdom. He is
> the one who will build a house for my Name,
> and I will establish the throne of his kingdom
> forever."[101]

The coming Messiah would be a human being ... who would be a descendant of Abraham through his son Isaac ... then Jacob ... then Judah ... down to King David. From that point on, he would be a Jew in the family line of King David.

THE COMING MESSIAH ... WHERE?

The place where the Messiah was to be born was specifically predicted by the prophet Micah in about 700 BC.[102] He wrote:

> "But you, Bethlehem Ephrathah, though you are small among the clans of Judah, out of you will come for Me one who will be Ruler over Israel, whose origins are from of old, from ancient times ... He will stand and shepherd his flock in the strength of the LORD, in the majesty of the name of the LORD his God, and they will live securely, for then his greatness will reach to the ends of the earth. And he will be their peace."

The Messiah was to be a direct descendant of Israel's King David who would be born in David's hometown of Bethlehem. He would not be a normal child, however. His divine nature is hinted at by the words, "whose origins are from of old, from ancient times." And the impact of his life is also clearly stated – "his greatness will reach to the ends of the earth. And he will be their peace."

THE COMING MESSIAH ... WHEN?

One of the most crucial elements for identifying who this future Deliverer would be is not only knowing his family line and where he would be born, but also determining *when* he would live.

The arrival of the future Deliverer was predicted in a general way when Jacob blessed his son Judah. He explained that,

"The scepter will not depart from Judah, nor the ruler's staff from between his feet, until he comes to whom it belongs and the obedience of the nations is his."[103]

The ruling staff was finally removed from Judah when the Jewish ruling council was abolished and the nation ceased to exist at the destruction of Jerusalem in AD 70. Thus, the Messiah was to come at some point prior to, and not too distant from, that time.

In the Biblical book of Daniel, written about 530 BC, the time in history when the Messiah would come was predicted much more specifically.

Daniel was from one of Israel's ruling families who had been taken captive to Babylon by Nebuchadnezzar prior to the Fall of Jerusalem in 586 BC. He was noted for his wisdom, skill and strong character, and became a highly respected and influential counselor to the kings of Babylon and later Persia. The Magi from the East who came to Jerusalem at the time of Jesus' birth searching for the one who was to be king of the Jews were members of an important group of men who had at one time been headed by Daniel.

Daniel wrote of the time of the Messiah's death, telling of an Anointed One who would put an end to sacrifice and offering, and be "cut off" in the process.[104]

Much discussion has taken place in scholarly circles over the years in efforts to identify specific details of this prophecy, and several possible dates have been suggested for the fulfillment of the various events. From our perspective over two dozen centuries later, this is to be expected. We have only incomplete records of ancient events. Calendars and means of reckoning time have changed dramatically from then until now. We live in a completely different cultural context. And we must work through translations of languages that are no longer spoken.

However, almost all scholars agree that the prophecy relates directly to some point in the life of Jesus of Nazareth – His birth, His baptism, His transfiguration, His triumphal entry into Jerusalem, or the date of His crucifixion. For our purpose of identifying *when* the One referred to as the "Anointed One" in the prophecy would come and be cut off, all that is really needed is to know the end date of the prophecy.

ISAAC NEWTON'S INTERPRETATION

Sir Isaac Newton is known worldwide as one of the

most brilliant scholars and scientists who ever lived. What is much less known about him is that he was also a deeply religious man who saw the hand of God in all things. In fact, Newton wrote more on religion than he did on natural science. In one of his books, *Observations upon the Prophecies of Daniel and the Apocalypse of St. John*, Newton specifically addressed Daniel's prophecy regarding when the Messiah would be "cut off."[105]

For Newton, the prophecy referred to 490 years from the decree to rebuild Jerusalem to the time of the crucifixion of Christ. He had an extensive knowledge of ancient history and identified the decree as occurring in the year 458 BC. Depending on whether the prophecy began when Ezra left Babylon or when he arrived in Jerusalem to start building, he offered two dates for when the crucifixion was prophesied to occur – AD 33 or AD 34.[106] One of the two dates generally accepted by scholars for the crucifixion of Christ on our modern calendars is Friday April 3, AD 33.[107]

THE COMING MESSIAH ... HOW?

One of the most amazing predictions concerning the coming Messiah that certainly adds an element of confirmation is that he would be born of a virgin. That would definitely be a unique way to fulfill the prophecy to Eve that the Deliverer would be the offspring of the *woman*. In about 735 BC, the prophet Isaiah gave a sign to the house of David:

> "The virgin will be with child and will give birth to a son, and will call him Immanuel ... For to us a child is born, to us a son is given, and the government will be on his shoulders. And he will be called Wonderful Counselor, Mighty God, Everlasting Father, Prince of Peace. Of the increase of his government and peace there will be no end. He will reign on David's throne and over his kingdom, establishing and upholding it with justice and righteousness from that time on and forever."[108]

This child who would be born of a virgin will be called Immanuel (which means, "God with us"), Wonderful Counselor, Mighty God, Everlasting Father, and Prince of Peace. The length of his reign on David's throne would be "from that time on and forever." He would clearly not be an ordinary child! All of those titles have been applied to Jesus by his followers who claim to be part of his everlasting kingdom.

The virgin birth was a powerful way to place an unmistakable, supernatural stamp of authority on the Messiah's identity. It was vitally important theologically to assure that the Messiah who would come to redeem mankind would be able to uniquely identify with the human race, and it was also a way to fulfill two seemingly contradictory Old Testament prophecies.

A BLESSING IN A CURSE

The prophet Jeremiah wrote at a time when the nation of Judah was about to be defeated by the Babylonian Empire and its people exiled to Babylon. He prophesied to the nation concerning the then king of Judah – a man named Jehoiachin, who ruled in Jerusalem for only 3 months and 10 days.

"Is this man Jehoiachin a despised, broken pot, an object no one wants? Why will he and his children be hurled out, cast into a land they do not know? O land, land, land, hear the word of the LORD! This is what the LORD says: 'Record this man as if childless, a man who will not prosper in his lifetime, for none of his offspring will prosper, none will sit on the throne of David or rule anymore in Judah.'"[109]

God had promised King David that the Messiah would be one of his direct descendants who would prosper and rule on his throne over an everlasting kingdom. But God made it clear here to Jehoiachin, David's descendant and legitimate successor, that *none* of his descendants would prosper and rule on David's throne. Thus, a great dilemma suddenly arose. The Messiah had to be the physical descendant of David and heir to David's throne, but he could not be the physical descendant of Jehoiachin, David's rightful heir.

Interestingly, both Joseph and Mary – Jesus' earthly parents – were descended from King David. The line of Joseph, the "father" of Jesus, is recorded in chapter 1 of the book of Matthew in the New Testament. The line of Mary, Jesus' mother, is found in Luke, chapter 3.

Joseph was the direct descendant of David through David's son Solomon, and later Jehoiachin. Joseph would have been the legitimate ruler of his people had they been allowed to place the rightful king on the throne during the Roman era. Mary, Jesus' mother, was also the direct descendant of David. However, she was descended from David through another of his sons, Nathan. Nathan was *not* a descendant of Jehoiachin.

Jesus was the physical descendant of David through his mother, Mary. And He was the legal heir to the throne of David through His adopted father, Joseph. In a very remarkable way, the virgin birth assured that the specific prophecies relating to the lineage of the coming Messiah would be precisely fulfilled. Because he was not the biological son of Joseph, Jesus was not subject to the curse placed on the physical descendants of Jehoiachin.

THE COMING MESSIAH ... WHAT AND WHY?

The question of what the Messiah would be like and why he would come has been the object of great debate between Christians and Jews for the last 2,000 years. Both agree that the Messiah will come as a Ruler. But Christians point out a second aspect of the Messiah's identity – He would first come as a Suffering Servant who would die at the hands of sinful men in order to redeem mankind from the curse of sin and death.

Nowhere in the Bible is this more clearly stated than in the book of Isaiah, chapter 53, written about 700 years before Jesus was born. It speaks clearly of the kind of death the Messiah would die, and the implications of that death for mankind.[110] To anyone familiar with the account of Jesus' crucifixion and resurrection, this passage seems like it must have been written *after* the event, not 700 years before it.

Jesus was "despised and rejected by men, a man of sorrows, and familiar with suffering." He was "pierced for our transgressions." He was "oppressed and afflicted, yet he did not open his mouth." He "was led like a lamb to the slaughter." He was "cut off from the land of the living," and "assigned a grave with the wicked, and with the rich in his death, though he had done no violence." After the "suffering of his soul," He saw "the light of life." He "poured out his life unto death." And He "bore the sin of many, and made intercession for the transgressors."

Over 20 centuries have passed since Gamaliel advised the Jewish leaders of his day to be cautious in their treatment of Peter and John, because if God was in it, they wouldn't be able to stop it. Today, more than two and a half billion people worldwide profess to be followers of Jesus the Messiah. A powerful indication, indeed, that what the early disciples were proclaiming was not from man, but from God.

6

IS THE BIBLE OF TODAY THE SAME AS THE ORIGINAL?

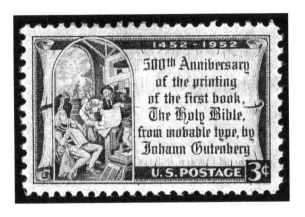

Midway through the Second Millennium, the world was forever changed when Johannes Gutenberg ushered in the era of mass communication where information could be communicated widely and rapidly as never before. Prior to his invention, Bibles had to be painstakingly copied by hand which could take a scribe a year to complete. As a result, only monasteries, museums and wealthy individuals could acquire one. The printing press changed that.

The system Gutenberg introduced incorporated a number of revolutionary ideas. He used metal instead of wood. He invented an oil-based instead of water-based ink that would adhere to metal and transfer easily to vellum or paper. He printed his materials using a large mechanical press. And he created moveable type where each letter, number, character or punctuation was its own metal block and could be moved and reused to make mass-printed books, leaflets, newspapers, posters and other printed items possible.

As the inscription on the 1952 commemorative U.S. postage stamp pictured above indicates, the first major work printed on Gutenberg's press was a copy of The Holy Bible. About 180 copies of the Gutenberg Bible were printed. Each had 1,286 pages with approximately 2,500 pieces of type per page. It's also known as the Forty-Two Line Bible because the pages were printed with two columns of 42 lines each. Only 49 copies are known to exist today. Of that number, only 21 are complete.[111]

Gutenberg's Press is one of the most significant inventions in the history of the world, and Johannes Gutenberg himself is ranked by some as the most important person of the last 1,000 years.[112] And yet, very little is actually known about him.

We don't really know when he was born, whether

or not he was married, if he had any children or where he is buried. Most of the information about him comes from legal and financial documents related to a sizeable debt he incurred when he began working on his Bible project. Shortly after the project was completed, the man who loaned him the money sued him in court, won the case and received the printing equipment and half of the Bibles as a settlement. Gutenberg later opened a second print shop, but it's unlikely he ever profited financially from his most important work.[113]

People will sometimes agree that the original Bible may have been God's Word, but they wonder if what has been transmitted to us down through the centuries is an accurate copy of what was originally given. After all, isn't it inevitable that major errors would creep into a text that was copied by hand for thousands of years, at least up to the time when printing presses entered the scene?

HOW WAS THE BIBLE PASSED ON TO US?

The basic answer to the question of how the Bible was copied by hand is, *very carefully!*

The original texts of the Bible were *not* passed along orally from generation to generation for centuries until they were finally written down, as is commonly understood and often erroneously taught. They were committed to writing by their authors and faithfully copied by people who were convinced that these documents were the divinely inspired words of the Creator of all things.

The closing comments in the last book of the Bible, the book of Revelation, express well the sentiments of those who carefully copied the various texts down through the ages.

"I warn everyone who hears the words of the prophecy of this book: If anyone adds anything to them, God will add to them the plagues described in this book. And if anyone takes words away from this book of prophecy, God will take away from him his share in the tree of life and in the holy city, which are described in this book."[114]

These books did not become divinely inspired writings because some religious group or council declared them to be so. From the outset, they were given to a group of people the Creator had purposely set apart to be caretakers of His message to mankind. As such, they were divinely *inspired* by God as He worked supernaturally through various individuals so that the resulting writings communicated exactly what He intended. They were *set apart* by Him through various signs, wonders and miracles so that the books and their authors bore His unique stamp of authority.

And they were *recognized* by the people for what they really were.

WHO COPIED THE HEBREW MANUSCRIPTS?

Until the invention of the printing press, copies of the Bible, like all other ancient documents, had to be made by hand. The people who did the copying were called "scribes." In Hebrew, the term is *sopher*, which means "to count." They were the detail-oriented accountants of their day who made lists and kept track of important documents, the most important of which were the texts of the Bible.

In ancient Egypt and Mesopotamia, the only people who were able to read and write were the scribes, in part because the Egyptian hieroglyphs and the cuneiform writing of Mesopotamia were difficult and complex. However, at the time of the Exodus from Egypt, when the first five books of the Bible were written by Moses, the simple 22-letter Hebrew alphabet began to be used. For the first time, ordinary people had the opportunity to read and write, and in Israel every man was commanded to read.[115]

The role of the scribe in ancient Israel was different from those in other cultures. Their job was to faithfully copy any writing exactly as it was given, and over the years, rigorous guidelines were developed for writing Biblical scrolls. In fact, the Talmud contains an entire treatise devoted to the very specific rules for the writing materials to be used, the size and dimensions of the scrolls to be made, and the size of the columns and lines of each scroll.[116]

Between the 5th and 10th centuries, a special group of scribes were designated by the name *Masoretes*, or "Masters of Tradition."[117] It is from that word that we get the term *Masoretic* text for the Hebrew copies of the Old Testament. Scribes were to study the texts of the Bible and carefully copy them for the generations to come.

Because it was so expensive and time consuming to make copies of manuscripts, two kinds of manuscripts would be circulated. Some were official copies made for the Temple and synagogues, while others were transcribed for private use. Many people, especially those in distant parts of the land, chose not to go to Jerusalem and pay the heavy price to have a copy made directly from the official text. These people would content themselves to have copies made from one possessed by the local leaders. The private copies were made carefully, but not with the meticulous care that characterized the official copies. They were obviously less expensive, but adequate for most uses.

HOW WERE THE MANUSCRIPTS COPIED?

The scribes who copied the official manuscripts of the

Biblical texts were convinced that these texts were, indeed, the Word of the Living God. As a result, no other documents in history have had the phenomenal degree of care taken to copy them. Rules were set for copying Synagogue manuscripts that assured that very few, if any, mistakes would ever be made. Looking at some of those rules will reveal why they were able to accomplish in large measure what they were intending to do.[118]

1. Official manuscripts had to be copied on *scrolls*, never *codices* which had pages like our modern books. The reason for this is quite clear to anyone who has ever seen an old or well-worn book. It's not difficult to have the binding break on one of these books and find pages falling out. By copying on a scroll, there is never any danger of losing a page. Everything is written continuously from beginning to end.

2. Official manuscripts had to be copied on parchment made from the skin of a clean animal. Papyrus, similar to modern paper, was not allowed until much later because of its less durable nature.

3. The text had to be written in black, erasable

ink. The reason for this rule is less obvious, but vitally important to the job of copying. Scribes needed to be able to make corrections when an error was made so that the whole scroll did not have to be rewritten. There was a limit, however, on the number of corrections allowed in any one manuscript.

4. Not even a single letter was allowed to be written without the scribe looking first at the manuscript being copied, and then copying it to the new scroll. Although common literature could be copied by one man reading the text while several others wrote down what they heard, this was expressly forbidden for the official copies of the Scriptures.

5. After the scribes completed their copies, they had to check their work. In order to make sure that the copies were made correctly, the total number of individual letters, words, verses and parashas (similar to our paragraphs) had to be counted, and the middle letter, word and verse determined. If they were off by even one letter, they knew that a mistake had occurred which needed to be found and corrected.

6. If any errors were found, the manuscript had

to be corrected within 30 days after it was written in order to assure that no uncorrected copies would be mistaken for corrected copies.

7. If four errors occurred on any one page, the entire manuscript had to be destroyed.

8. Special factors such as unusual size or placement were carefully noted and copied exactly as they were in the master copy.

9. If the king walked in and addressed the scribe while he was writing the name for God, the scribe must take no notice of the king until after he had written the name.

INTERESTING FOOTNOTES

Once the manuscripts began to be printed, many of the notes and unusual characteristics were kept as part of the text in copies of the printed Hebrew Old Testament. Some of them are particularly interesting.

For example, if you were to read the Aramaic footnotes at the end of the book of Deuteronomy in a Hebrew Bible, you would learn that the total number of verses in that book is 955. You would also learn that the total number of verses in the first five books of the Old Testament, called the Torah, is 5,845, and the total number of words in the Torah is 97,856. The total number of letters making up those first five books is 400,945.

Leviticus 8:8 has a footnote mentioning that it is the middle verse in the Hebrew Torah. Leviticus 10:16 contains the middle word, and Leviticus 11:42 contains the middle letter of the first five books of the Hebrew Bible. Isaiah 17:3 is the middle verse of the Prophets.

Because the scribes were very concerned to pass along to the next generation a text that was exactly like the one they received, they took meticulous care to note anything unusual. It may not have been important, but they noted it just in case. One letter in Genesis 2:4 is written smaller than the others. The footnote at that verse mentions that it is to be copied exactly that way. Psalm 80:14 contains one of four raised letters. These letters are written above the others in a way similar to a superscript. The other raised letters occur in Job 38:13 & 15, and in Judges 18:30.

One particularly interesting footnote is for a letter similar to our lowercase English "l" in Numbers 25:12. If you look very closely at that particular letter, you will notice a tiny crack in it. The footnote explains that this letter is cracked and must be copied that way. Apparently, a scribe somewhere along the line noticed that the letter was like that in the text he was copying, and he noted that fact so all future scribes would be aware of it. The word in which the crack appears is the word, "shalom," the Hebrew word for "peace."

WHAT KINDS OF "ERRORS" DID THE SCRIBES MAKE?

It's the nature of language to make subtle changes in word usage and spelling over time. The English language from the time of William Shakespeare or the King James Bible is significantly different from the English language of today. "Publick" is now "public." "Honour" is now "honor." We don't "wax eloquent" anymore. Today, we "wax" our cars!

The vast majority of the supposed "errors" that are found in the Biblical texts are not errors at all. They are primarily updates in spelling or changes in the names of places. In a similar way, Cape Canaveral in Florida became Cape Kennedy after the assassination of President John F. Kennedy in the early 1960's, and was later changed back to Cape Canaveral.

In 1947, one of the greatest archaeological discoveries in the history of Biblical research was made with the finding of the Dead Sea Scrolls. Prior to this discovery, the oldest actual manuscript of the Old Testament that was known dated from AD 980. The Dead Sea Scrolls dated from at least 100 BC. With their discovery, scholars had the opportunity for the very first time to actually look at copies of the same texts that were made 1,000 years apart, and check to see how accurately the Bible had been copied by hand during that 1,000 year time.

Scholars were amazed to discover that the text of Isaiah from the Dead Sea Scrolls proved to be word-for-word identical to our standard Hebrew Bible in more than 95% of the cases. The other 5% were primarily obvious slips of the pen, and updates in spelling, word usage and place names.[119] That is even more amazing when it's understood that the Dead Sea Scrolls were not official copies. Many of the Scrolls were clearly quick copies made by students.

HOW ABOUT THE NEW TESTAMENT?

The material in existence today for establishing the integrity of the text for the Hebrew Old Testament is many times greater than the material for establishing the text of any other ancient document, except the New Testament.

There exist today 5,795 known copies of the complete or fragmented manuscripts of the Greek New Testament dating from 30 to 150 years from the events they record, with the earliest copy dated AD 117 and a few others that are possibly from the first century still under review. In addition, there are 7,974 manuscripts in other languages such as Armenian, Coptic, and Syriac dating from 100-150 years from the events, and more than 10,000 copies of the earliest

Latin translation dated about 300-350 years after the New Testament books were written.[120] These other translations are helpful for checking the meaning and accuracy of various words or passages in the Greek New Testament.

In addition to the more than 25,000 early New Testament manuscripts and translations, there are thousands of references to the New Testament writings in other ancient documents and artifacts, bringing the total number of references to about 66,000.[121]

To put those numbers in context, we currently have about 1000 copies of the works of Aristotle, with the earliest copy dating around 1,200 years after it was written. There are 210 copies of Plato's *Tetralogies*, with the earliest copy written about 1,200 years after Plato lived. Caesar's firsthand account of the Gallic Wars has 251 manuscripts currently in existence, with the earliest copy written about 900 years after the events they recorded. The ancient document with the closest number of manuscripts to the New Testament is the *Iliad* by Homer recounting the Trojan War. 1,757 manuscripts have survived to date, with the oldest copy dating 400 years from the events.[122]

Is the Bible of today an accurate reflection of what was originally written? The answer is a resounding, "Yes!" And it certainly seems reasonable to expect that if the Creator actually did choose to communicate to mankind in the form of a document or documents, He would have made sure that those documents were transmitted accurately as copies were made from generation to generation.

SO, WHAT'S IT ALL ABOUT, ANYWAY?

WANTED :

JESUS CHRIST

Alias: The Messiah. The Son Of God. King Of Kings Lord Of Lords. Prince Of Peace. Etc.

- Notorious leader of an underground liberation movement

- Wanted for the following charges:
  —Practicing medicine, winemaking and food distribution without a license.
  —Interfering with businessmen in the temple.
  —Associating with known criminals, radicals, subversives, prostitutes and street people.
  —Claiming to have the authority to make people into God's children.

APPEARANCE: Typical hippie type—long hair, beard, robe, sandals.
> Hangs around slum areas, few rich friends, often sneaks out into the desert.
BEWARE: This man is extremely dangerous. His insidiously inflammatory message is particularly dangerous to young people who haven't been taught to ignore him yet. He changes men and claims to set them free.

WARNING: HE IS STILL AT LARGE!

This Wanted poster was originally published in a Christian underground newspaper and later mentioned in a news article about the Jesus Movement in the June 21, 1971 issue of TIME magazine.[123]

At the height of the Counterculture Revolution of the 1960s with its focus on "drugs, sex and rock 'n roll," there suddenly appeared, almost out of nowhere, a group of people who came to be known as the Jesus People, or Jesus Freaks. The movement exploded across the United States, Canada, Europe and Central America into the 1980s. It cut across almost all social and religious dividing lines. Youth with crew cuts hung out with long-haired hippies. Ivy League preppies prayed and sang alongside construction workers and college dropouts. Catholics and Jews visited Protestant churches. And Protestants found themselves talking with nuns and openly enjoying Mass.

Christian music saw a radical change from staid hymns accompanied by an organ or piano to the pulsating guitar and drum rock music of the street people who now wrote lyrics with a strongly Christian message. One of the most visible events of the Jesus Movement was a conference held in Dallas, TX with nightly gatherings in the Cotton Bowl. Explo '72 drew 85,000 young people. Most were from the US, but the conference included an international representation from 75 countries.[124] The concluding event was an eight-hour-long Christian music festival that drew an estimated attendance of 100,000-200,000 people.[125]

The Movement primarily sought a return to the vibrant faith of the early Christians. Their message? The Bible is true. Miracles happen. God really did so love the world that He gave His only begotten Son.[126]

If the Bible really is the record of the Creator's special communication to mankind, then the next question to ask ourselves is, "What is the basic message of the Bible? What has the Creator chosen to tell us about Himself, His creation, and His relationship with us?"

As we prepare to answer that question, there are some misconceptions about Biblical faith that need to be addressed.

BIBLICAL FAITH

First, true Biblical faith is *intelligent* faith, not *irrational* faith.

The Bible does not encourage its readers to put their minds on a shelf and just "believe." Rather, it teaches us to love the Lord our God with all our hearts, all our souls, all our *minds*, and all our strength. Those who embrace the Bible's teaching are told to *study*, to prepare their *minds* for action, and always be prepared to give an *answer* to everyone who asks them to give the reason for the hope that is in them. The Bible encourages its readers to think, and think clearly.

Second, the faith encouraged in the Bible is a faith rooted in *history*, not *philosophy*.

The events mentioned in the Bible actually occurred in time and space. There really was a Noah, who really built an ark. The Israelites under Joshua really did walk around the city of Jericho and see the walls of the city collapse when they blew their ram's horn trumpets. The "historical Jesus" and the Jesus of the Bible are one and the same. Jesus really was born of a virgin. He really did walk on water. He really did rise from the dead. The Bible does not allow for a discontinuity between facts and faith. Inherent in the system is the potential for it to be verified or falsified.

Third, true Biblical faith is an *objective* faith, not a *subjective* one.

The key for believers is not the amount of faith someone has, but the object of their faith. The issue is not whether you or I *believe* Jesus fed 5,000 men with five small barley loaves and two small fish. The issue is – *did it actually happen?*

WHO IS GOD?

The first three chapters of the first book of the Bible, the book of Genesis, provide an excellent introduction to the Bible's overall message.

The book begins with a declaration of who God is. He is the One who created the heavens and the earth by simply willing them into existence. He is not limited in any way in power or authority. Rather, He is the Creator and Ruler of all that exists.

In contrast to some other theological or philosophical systems, the Bible does not teach that there is a dualism in the universe where equal powers of Good and Evil are at war with one another. It also does not teach that God is simply a part of the material universe, or the consciousness of the universe. He is the Creator and absolute, sovereign Ruler over all things.

As the rest of the Bible unfolds, more of the nature of God is revealed through His dealings with mankind.

For example, the destruction of Sodom and Gomorrah shows that He is a God who judges sin. The events surrounding the exodus from Egypt point to the fact that He is the One who rules over the kings of the earth, and delivers His people from bondage. The Levitical laws teach us that He establishes specific requirements for worship. When Moses stands before the burning bush and is ordered to take off his sandals, we learn that He is One whose holiness demands reverence in His presence. When Jonah is sent to preach to the wicked city of Nineveh, we see that He is merciful and deeply concerned about the ultimate well-being of all mankind.

People today will often talk about God, but the God they talk about too often bears little resemblance to the One, all-powerful, all-knowing, holy, just, loving, personal Creator of all things that the Bible reveals. I remember asking a friend some time ago if he believed in God. His response was, "Of course, I believe in God ... I am God!" I can assure you as one who knew this person well – if what he said were true, we would all be in a lot of trouble!

WHY DID HE CREATE?

The account in Genesis goes on to explain God's intended purpose for creation, and, in particular, God's intended purpose for mankind.

When He had finished His work of creating, God surveyed all that He had made and pronounced it "very good." Everything had been created to be in perfect harmony and peace, with mankind experiencing intimate communion with God and ruling responsibly over the created order. The first created human being, Adam, exercised this responsible rule by carefully studying the nature of the animals God had created in order to give them appropriate names. He also worked in and took care of the Garden of Eden in which he had been placed. Adam, in turn, was to demonstrate His submission to God's rule by honoring a very simple restriction.

Adam was given permission to partake of the fruit from all of the trees in the Garden ... except one. This one tree, located in the middle of the Garden and called "the tree of the knowledge of good and evil" would serve as a test. Would Adam submit to the authority of his Creator and refrain from eating from that one tree? Or, would he disobey and eat from the tree, even though he had been told that the consequence of his disobedience would be his and his wife's physical deaths?

The tree was appropriately named. If Adam obeyed God and refused to eat from the tree, he would understand the difference between good and evil from the perspective of one who had chosen to do what was right or good. If he disobeyed God and ate from the tree, he would understand the difference between good and evil from the perspective of one who had chosen to do what was wrong or evil.

People often think of "evil" as something that is grossly wicked, or terribly bad. But that's not what evil is from a Biblical perspective. According to one dictionary definition that is actually close to the Biblical understanding, evil is "anything which impairs the happiness of a being or deprives a being of any good."[127] From a Biblical perspective, evil does not have to be terribly bad. Rather, it's anything that impairs happiness or deprives of some good. Evil is something that is less than the best. It is second best, or worse.

A computer virus is a good illustration of how evil operates. Whether you're a computer expert or consider yourself someone who is technologically challenged, you probably know that it's a good idea to protect your computer by installing an anti-virus program. A computer virus is a type of malicious code or program that alters the way a computer was designed to operate. In the process, it has the potential to cause unexpected or damaging effects.[128] Some computer viruses are just a nuisance. Others can completely destroy a computer's ability to function.

Because God is infinite and perfect, His desire for those He created is that they experience the very best. Anything that falls short of the perfection He desires is less than the best. Ultimately, like an aggressive computer virus, if evil were allowed to continue unchecked, the whole creation would eventually be completely corrupted.

When Adam chose to disobey God, the harmony and peace that God intended was marred. He was not fit to rule and was driven out of the Garden. In accordance with what God had said, the sentence of death was passed. And Adam ended his days by returning to the dust from which he was made.

WHY DO WE NEED A SAVIOR?

The rest of the Bible records how pervasive this tendency to choose evil is in the heart of mankind. Very quickly, God's command to cleave to one wife was violated by polygamy, then adultery, then rape and incest. Adam's son Cain murdered his brother Abel. The worship of idols made in the image of created things took the place of the worship of God, the Creator.

Even the "righteous" were plagued by this tendency to do what is evil. Noah got drunk shortly after his deliverance from the Flood. Abraham lied in an effort to protect his life. David, the man after God's own heart, committed adultery and arranged for the death of the woman's husband.

Our modern society often equates evil with pleasure. It's seen as the satisfaction that comes from doing something "my way." But in doing so, we fail to see its true nature as something that is ultimately harmful to ourselves and others. The examples and teaching recorded throughout the Bible show clearly that turning away from God results in the perversion of what God intended. It causes pain. It enslaves one to destructive habits. And it keeps people from reaching their full potential by turning them away from the unique purposes for which they were created.

One of the clearest areas in which this pervasive tendency to sin can be seen in our day is the distortion of one of God's greatest gifts. *Lust* has replaced *love* as the driving force in many intimate relationships. As a result, people forsake the secure and loving atmosphere God designed for marriage and the family in order to pursue adulterous and promiscuous lifestyles. In our generation, this has led to rampant divorce, venereal diseases of epidemic proportions, AIDS, and widespread child abuse.

HOW DID GOD DEAL WITH THE PROBLEM?

When sin entered the world, God was not taken by surprise! He knew what Adam and the rest of mankind would do from before the foundations of the world. As soon as the event occurred, God instituted a plan for restoring mankind to fellowship and right standing with Himself.

When God spoke to Adam, Eve, and the serpent in the Garden after they had eaten the forbidden fruit, He briefly explained the consequences of their actions, and also made a subtle allusion to the fact that someday God would raise up a Deliverer who would restore what had been lost. Sin and death would be defeated. Their hold on mankind would be broken.

This promised salvation would come through a descendant of the woman who would one day decisively crush the head of the serpent, and be struck in the heel in the process. The subsequent teaching of the

Bible gradually reveals that the promised Deliverer will actually be God Himself, who would come to earth as the Deliverer, Restorer and Savior of mankind. The fullness of this is brought into clear focus in the life, death, and resurrection of Jesus Christ.

WHY DIDN'T GOD JUST DO IT, AND GET IT OVER WITH?

If the Creator's plan from the beginning was to provide salvation and restoration for all mankind, why didn't He just come and do it after Adam rebelled? It certainly would have been a lot easier and taken a lot less time! What was going on with the establishment of the nation of Israel, the system of sacrifices, the tabernacle and Temple, and the events of Biblical history?

The Hebrew Scriptures contain the specific record of God's communication to mankind prior to the coming of Christ. In it, He both *records* important information, and *reveals* important information. For example, the Bible *records* the serpent's lie in the Garden of Eden, Cain's murder of his brother, and David's adultery. It *reveals*, however, that lying, murder and adultery are wrong. The events are recorded along with their consequences to provide examples of what happens when God's principles are either followed or not followed.

Through that revelation, God laid a foundation for

a proper understanding of the Person and work of the coming Deliverer. As with any drama, the "set" helps us understand the context and meaning of the story. In a similar way, the events and teaching recorded and set forth in the teaching of the Hebrew Scriptures set the stage for correctly recognizing who the promised Deliverer would be, and what He would be doing when He came.

The "clean and unclean" laws taught that one must be *cleansed* from sin in order to enter into God's presence. The killing of animals showed that sin leads ultimately to death. The specific requirements and duties of the high priest pointed to the fact that a special mediator was required to intercede between God and man in order to offer the acceptable sacrifice.

All these things, and many others, paved the way for understanding that Christ – the Messiah and Deliverer – was, in the words of John the Baptist, "the Lamb of God, who takes away the sin of the world." It also provided a unique and powerful way to authenticate the Bible's message, since no individual could counterfeit something woven into the fabric of the world's entire history.

WHAT DOES THE BIBLE SAY TO US?

People today often look to acts of penance, works of charity, meditation, reincarnation, or a whole host of

other things as the means by which they will somehow make themselves worthy of gaining eternal life.
All their efforts, however, fall far short of the absolute
perfection that God requires.

It's like trying to jump across the Grand Canyon at
its widest point. One person may stumble and fall off
the edge. Another may start from a standing position
and leap five or ten feet. And a third may break all
world records for the long jump by running, jumping,
and somersaulting 35 or 40 feet out from the rim. All,
however, fall to the bottom of the canyon with their
feeble attempts being so far short of the goal as to not
even deserve mention. What is needed is some kind
of bridge that will enable us to get across the chasm.

God provided that bridge for mankind through
the Person of Jesus Christ, who is the Way, the Truth
and the Life. Through Christ, the promised Savior
and Deliverer, God provided a way for mankind's sin
to be forgiven, intimate communion with God to be
restored, and power for living to be made available to
those who turn to Him.

God is the Creator and Ruler of all things, and the
One to whom all creation owes its allegiance. People
are created beings that God designed to rule responsibly over the world, walking humbly before Him,
and enjoying intimate communion with Him in the
process.

A QUESTION FOR US

The Bible is a very complex book. Yet, its central message is really quite simple. When all is said and done, it teaches that God is real, and that each person has to answer the same question that Adam had to answer:

> "Who is going to be the 'boss' in your life? You, someone or something else, or God who created you?"

Will you and I submit to God and His plan for our lives, or will we decide that our own ideas are better and say "no" to Him? God desires the best for each of us – in this world, and in the world to come. He doesn't settle for second best. And He never gives up!

Biblical faith is confidence that God can be trusted to do what He has said He will do. He told Adam, Eve and the Serpent that He would one day send a Savior and Deliverer to defeat sin and death. It would not be something that we humans would do. It would be something that God Himself would do.

The basic message of the Bible can actually be summed up simply in the words of the apostle Paul in Romans 6:23,

> "For the wages of sin is death, but the gift of God is eternal life in Christ Jesus our Lord."

8

WHAT'S THE DIFFERENCE?

"I'm not religious. I'm spiritual."

That remark, seen on a t-shirt proudly worn by a young millennial, echoes the thinking of about 26% of American adults.[129] In fact, the number has grown enough in the recent past to give the group a name. They used to be called "religiously unaffiliated." Now, because of their answer to the question on surveys – "What is your religious tradition?" – they have a new name.

They're called "nones."

The largest group who identify as "nones" are under 30 years old, unmarried with no children.[130] About 30% of young men place themselves in that category, compared to about 23% of young women.[131] Although they don't identify with any particular church, synagogue, mosque or temple, they are generally not atheists. About 90% say they believe in some kind of higher power, and 56% say they believe in God as described in the Bible.[132]

In recent years, it's become increasingly socially acceptable to be a "none," which is one reason why the percentage of those who say they are religiously unaffiliated has risen significantly. However, once people enter their 30s, the tendency is to return to a more organized religious tradition.[133] But which one?

It's at this point that the question naturally arises. "Don't all religions teach the same thing, anyway?"

While it's true that there are definite similarities in terms of the ethical teachings of the major religions of the world, there are also a number of very significant differences. As the outspoken mayor of one prominent U.S. city allegedly said, "Why should I turn the other cheek? I'm not a Christian!"

The focus of the Bible is on who God is, what He has done, and what His will is for mankind. And its message is very distinctive.

THE NATURE OF MANKIND

Two important questions arise in any philosophical inquiry about the nature of mankind.

The first is, "Why is mankind so noble?"

Why is it not unusual to hear of heroic deeds done by individuals who are willing to risk their lives to go to the aid of others with no interest in or expectation of personal gain. For example, of the 2,977 victims who were killed in the World Trade Center towers in New York City on September 11, 2001, 412 were emergency workers who rushed into the burning towers to try to save people they didn't even know.[134]

The Biblical explanation for why people can do such valiant deeds is that human beings are uniquely created in the image of God and thus capable of doing wonderful acts of courage, bravery and charity.

"Then God said, 'Let us make man in our image, in our likeness, and let them rule over the fish of the sea and the birds of the sky, over the livestock and all the earth, and over all the creatures that move along the ground.' So God created man in his own image, in the image of God he created him; male and female he created them."[135]

The second question that must be asked is, "Why is mankind so cruel?"

The genocide of European Jews during the Holocaust of World War II systematically murdered about two-thirds of Europe's Jewish population in pogroms, mass shootings, through work in concentration camps, and in gas chambers and gas vans in extermination camps. Millions of others, including ethnic Poles, Soviet civilians and prisoners of war,

Gypsies, the handicapped, political and religious dissidents, and homosexual men were also persecuted and killed by Nazi Germany and its collaborators.[136]

The Biblical answer for how this horrendous evil could occur is that the natural tendency of our fallen human nature is to turn from good to pursue self-centered goals. While other religious teaching often sees mankind as basically good at heart when uncorrupted by outside influences, the Bible clearly teaches that mankind, left on its own, has a natural tendency toward evil.

"There is no one righteous, not even one; there is no one who understands, no one who seeks God. All have turned away, they have together become worthless; there is no one who does good, not even one."[137]

"For from within, out of men's hearts, come evil thoughts, sexual immorality, theft, murder, adultery, greed, malice, deceit, lewdness, envy, slander, arrogance and folly. All these evils come from inside and make a man 'unclean.'"[138]

In contrast to most other religious literature, the Bible not only tells of the strengths of its major characters, it also tells of their sins. David's sin of adultery and murder is not glossed over or left unreported. Nor is Noah's drunkenness after the Flood, or the fact that Peter denied even knowing Jesus three times just prior to the crucifixion. The book of Judges shows very graphically how men left to do what is right in their own eyes will turn away from God and sink deeply into depravity.

Biblical faith sees the need for a transformation of the heart by the power of God, not just better education or a change in the environment. It's not unusual to walk into a Biblically based church and hear testimonies of people who have seen their lives transformed from within.

THE NATURE OF SALVATION

Another major characteristic of the Bible's message is that mankind comes into fellowship with God not because of something which an individual does, but because of something that God has done. One's right to enter God's presence is an unmerited gift.

Our actions and activities, no matter how difficult or noble or religious they may be, do not make us acceptable to God. The Bible teaches that no amount of meditation, or prayers, or acts of asceticism, or the performing of religious rituals will make us worthy enough to stand before Him. We don't find or discover God. God *reveals* Himself to us. We don't earn our way into His presence because of the good works that *we* do. He allows us into His presence because of the good work *He* has done.

I met a man several years ago who was reading from a little book. When I asked what he was doing, he informed me that he was praying. I asked how often he prayed, and he replied, "Not often. Only 5 times a day!" I was obviously quite impressed with his dedication.

As we talked, however, I learned that the book from which he was reading contained prayers that he was required to recite by his religion in order to make himself acceptable to the deity he worshipped. There was no sense of a personal relationship with God. He did not pray in order to talk with God about what was happening in his life, or to ask for guidance or wisdom. He prayed because he was required to pray to be accepted. He had been taught that if he performed his required duties often enough and well enough, he would earn the right to receive certain blessings.

Although our arrogant modern culture would have us believe that we deserve to be loved because we are somehow really good deep down inside, the truth is that we are not good, and we do not deserve God's blessings. Salvation is a gracious gift. John Newton's famous hymn captures the concept of grace extremely well:

"Amazing grace, how sweet the sound that saved a wretch like me. I once was lost, but now am found. Was blind, but now I see."

John Newton was not saved because he was a good person who found God. Prior to his conversion, he was a slave trader, a drunkard and a brawler. He was, in fact, a "wretch" who was "lost" and was "found" by God. Biblical Christianity teaches that good works are the *result* of salvation, not the means to it. When a person accepts what God has done on his behalf, God's Spirit empowers him. As we look to God, He graciously gives us the desire and power to do His will. When we pray, it is to have fellowship with God.

In the words of the apostle John, "We love because He first loved us."[139]

THE NATURE OF GOD

When I was a freshman in college, I took a required literature course that used the Bible as one of its texts because of its exceptional influence on history and the world. I was actually looking forward to taking the class because I had a lot of questions about the Bible and wondered if it was, in fact, true.

Unfortunately, the professor seemed to have as one of his goals for the course a desire to destroy what he considered the ignorant faith of some of his naïve students. In one of the classes, the professor correctly pointed out that the Hebrew word for God in the first verse of the Bible – *Elohim* – is a plural noun. He then went on to tell his students that the Bible actually began as a polytheistic document that over time evolved into a monotheistic document.

What this professor did *not* tell his students, whether because of personal ignorance or because he was intellectually dishonest, is that whenever *Elohim* is used for God in the Bible, it is followed by a *singular* verb.

That unusual grammatical construction highlights an often misunderstood, but key characteristic of the Biblical teaching about who God is. It's the idea that the one God who created all things exists in three Persons, or what theologians call the Trinity. It's a teaching that seeks to explain how two clearly revealed but seemingly contradictory truths fit together.

The Bible clearly teaches that there is only one God. When Moses delivered the Ten Commandments to the Israelites, he stressed this truth:

"Hear, O Israel, the LORD our God, the LORD
is one."[140]

The prophet Isaiah could not be clearer in his confirmation of this truth:

"I am the LORD, and there is no other; apart
from Me there is no God ... I am the LORD,

and there is no other ... there is no God apart from Me, a righteous God and a Savior; there is none but Me. Turn to Me and be saved, all you ends of the earth; for I am God, and there is no other."[141]

However, there are also indications throughout the Bible that at first suggest, and then clearly reveal that there is something very unique and very special about the singularity of this one God.

When God created mankind, He said: "Let *Us* make man in *our* image, in *our* likeness ..."[142]

God's comment after the Fall of Adam was: "The man has now become like one of *Us*, knowing good and evil ..."[143]

Other passages ascribe the attributes of deity to the Spirit of God, and to a Person known as the Angel of the LORD who appeared in bodily form to various individuals and spoke directly to them.

The full impact of these passages is brought into clearer view in the New Testament statements affirming the deity of Christ. The apostle John, for example, explains who Jesus Christ really is at the beginning of his gospel:

"In the beginning was the Word, and the Word was with God, and the Word was God."[144]

The apostle Paul in his letter to the Philippians affirmed what John wrote. Referring to Christ, he explained:

> "Who, being in very nature God, did not consider equality with God something to be grasped, but made Himself nothing, taking the very nature of a servant, being made in human likeness. And being found in appearance as a man, He humbled Himself and became obedient to death – even death on a cross!"[145]

The idea of something being one and at the same time having three dimensions should not strike us as particularly surprising. Existence itself is usually considered as having three elements – time, space and matter, and each of these three elements has three dimensions. Time is made up of the past, the present and the future. Space is made up of length, width and height. Matter exists in solid, liquid and gaseous states.

We should also not be surprised to learn that the nature of the infinite Creator of all things is beyond our ability as finite human beings to fully comprehend.

GOD LOVES YOU

It is not uncommon to see a bumper sticker on a car,

or some graffiti written on a wall somewhere that informs you that God loves you. It's so common that we rarely ponder its significance, but it's a distinctly Biblical message.

The great significance of this teaching is often completely overlooked. What the Bible is saying is that God *Himself* loves us and is our Savior. Unlike other religions, the Bible does not teach that God ultimately only sent messengers or prophets to tell us about Himself and provide some means to salvation. Rather, He Himself came into the world to save us. Jesus was not just a human or angelic messenger. He was God. God entered time and space to become a man and provide a way for mankind to be reconciled to its Creator.

God Loves You is an especially profound statement to those in polytheistic cultures where their gods clearly do *not* "love" their adherents. They tolerate them, at best, and must be appeased so they won't hurt their followers.

John Paton, a nineteenth century missionary to the South Sea Islands, saw this firsthand. He wrote of his experience:

"The Tannese had hosts of stone idols, charms, and sacred objects, which they abjectly feared, and in which they devoutly believed. They were given up to countless superstitions, and firmly glued to their dark heathen practices. Their worship was entirely a service of fear, its aim being to propitiate this or that evil spirit, to prevent calamity or to secure revenge … Sacred men and women, wizards and witches, received presents regularly to influence the gods and to remove sickness, or to cause it, by the Nahak, i.e. incantation over remains of food, or the skin of fruit, such as banana, which the person has eaten on whom they wished to operate.

"They also worshipped the spirits of departed ancestors and heroes, through their material idols of wood and stone, but chiefly of stone. They feared these spirits and sought their aid, especially seeking to propitiate those who presided over war and peace, famine and plenty, health and sickness, destruction and prosperity, life and death. Their whole worship was one of slavish fear; and, so far as ever I could learn, they had no idea of a God of mercy or grace."[146]

THE PERSON OF JESUS CHRIST

Jesus of Nazareth was born in an out-of-the-way

Middle Eastern village. He was an obscure carpenter. He never held a political or military office. He never wrote a book. He never traveled extensively. He was put to death as a criminal after His most committed followers deserted Him. Yet, the simple fact of the matter is that He has had a greater impact on the history of the world than any other person who has ever lived.

That truth is acknowledged every day on the front page of every major and minor daily newspaper. It's acknowledged every week and every month on the front covers of every major and minor magazine that is published on any subject. It's even acknowledged by the most ardent skeptic or atheist in each and every email or piece of personal correspondence that he or she sends out that contains a date on it that relates directly to the birth of Christ.

Unlike all other major religious leaders, Jesus did not claim to be a great prophet, showing mankind the way to peace and prosperity. He claimed to *be* the way. Unlike all other major religious leaders, Jesus did not point the attention of the people to God. He pointed the attention of the people to *Himself.* Jesus is the only major figure in history who ever *claimed* to be God, and the only person who ever lived who has convinced a significant portion of the world's population that He *is* God! Indeed, many of Jesus' statements about Himself would clearly be blasphemous if He were *not* God.

Jesus said:

> "Come to me, all you who are weary and burdened, and I will give you rest ... I am the Way, and the Truth, and the Life ... I and the Father are one ... Anyone who has seen me has seen the Father ... I am the bread of life ... If anyone is thirsty, let him come to me and drink. Whoever believes in me, as the Scripture has said, streams of living water will flow from within him ... I am the Light of the world ... I am the Good Shepherd ... I am the resurrection and the life. He who believes in me will live, even though he dies ..."[147]

SON OF GOD?

Have you ever wondered why Jesus would choose the phrase "Son of God" as a key reference to His deity. The phrase certainly had a very profound meaning for the Jews of His day because they understood it as a clear claim by Him to be God. That's why He was put to death.

In the interchange between Jesus and the Jewish leaders in John 10,

"Jesus said to them, 'I have shown you many
great miracles from the Father. For which of
these do you stone me?' 'We are not stoning
you for any of these,' replied the Jews, 'but for
blasphemy, because you, a mere man, claim to
be God.' Jesus answered them ... 'Why then do
you accuse me of blasphemy because I said, "I
am God's Son"?'"

After Pilate flogged Jesus and brought Him out
before the chief priests and their officials to let them
know that he could find no basis for a charge against
Him, they insisted,

"We have a law, and according to that law he
must die, because he claimed to be the Son of
God."

Sons often grow up to become wonderful young
men of whom their fathers are very proud. They
share many of their father's ideas. But not all. They
have many interests that are similar to their fathers.
But also interests that are different. They may even
sound a lot like their dads on the phone until people
listen long enough to realize the difference. Sons are
like their fathers in many ways, but they are not their
fathers. They're their father's sons. In a similar way,
Jesus calling Himself the "Son" of God doesn't seem

to equate with His claim to be God. So how does Jesus' being God's Son make Him God?

Phil Collins wrote the music and lyrics for the songs in the Disney animated feature, *Tarzan*. His lyrics to one of the songs provides an insight into how Jesus and the Jews of His day understood the meaning of "Son of."

In the animated film, there is a sequence where we see Tarzan growing from a weak little toddler who is barely able to keep up with the other apes into a strong and agile adult who becomes their leader. As we watch this transformation take place, the lyrics from one of the songs tell us who this child really is. Tarzan is "Son of Man."

In the context of the film, it is clear that he is unlike those with whom he grew up and among whom he lived. Although he was raised by the apes and lived with them, Tarzan was not an ape. He was a man. He was not an ape-kind of creature. He was a man-kind of creature. Tarzan was not Son of Ape. He was Son of Man.

Similarly, when Jesus told the Jewish leaders He was the *Son of God*, they understood exactly what He was saying to them. He was claiming divinity for Himself. He was saying, in essence, that He was God-kind of Being, not human or angelic kind of being.

Jesus also used the phrase "Son of Man" – because

He is also man-kind of being. After declaring at the beginning of his Gospel that the Word was God, John writes,

> "The Word became flesh and made his dwelling among us. We have seen his glory, the glory of the One and Only, who came from the Father, full of grace and truth."

The Nicene Creed expresses it well.

> "We believe in one Lord, Jesus Christ, the only Son of God, eternally begotten of the Father, God from God, light from light, true God from true God, begotten, not made, of one Being with the Father; through him all things were made. For us and for our salvation he came down from heaven, was incarnate of the Holy Spirit and the Virgin Mary and became truly human."

All religions do not teach the same things. In actual fact, they are very different from one another. The Biblical teaching about the nature of mankind, the nature of salvation, the nature of God, and the unique Person of Jesus Christ are just a few of the differences.

9

DID JESUS REALLY RISE FROM THE DEAD?

*"My name is Ozymandias, king of kings; Look
on my works, ye Mighty, and despair!"*

Those words from Percy Bysshe Shelley's famous poem *Ozymandias* were inscribed on the pedestal of a fallen, broken and partly buried statue of an ancient monarch, and stand in marked contrast to the humble words we noted earlier on the tomb of Cyrus the Great.[148] Interestingly, like Cyrus, Ozymandias was a real ancient monarch, and the inscription in the sonnet is a reference to a real event.

The name is the Greek form of part of the throne name for pharaoh Ramesses II of Egypt who ruled from 1279-1213 BC. He is often regarded as Egypt's greatest and most powerful pharaoh. He lived to be over 90 years old, reigned longer than any other ruler of Egypt, and won the most celebrated victory in Egyptian history – the Battle of Kadesh against the Hittites. A copy of the peace treaty he negotiated after the battle is displayed on the wall of the General Assembly building of the United Nations in New York.[149]

Ramesses sought to eternalize himself in stone. He erected temples, monuments and more colossal statues of himself than any other pharaoh. He even inscribed his own royal name on many existing statues. In 1816, an Italian archeologist named Giovanni Battista Belzoni removed the 7 ¼ ton head and torso fragment of a statue of this king from a temple Ramesses had built at Thebes in Egypt. Shelley wrote his poem a year later when he learned that the statue fragment had been acquired by the British Museum.[150]

The declaration in the poem about his greatness is a paraphrase based on a passage from the writings in Greek of the historian Diodorus Siculus that described a massive statue of Ramesses with this inscription:

"King of Kings Ozymandias am I. If any want to know how great I am and where I lie, let him outdo me in my work."

While he was alive, Ramesses took the title God and King, and created monuments, temples and buildings to promote himself as a living god.[151] When he died, his body was mummified and placed in an elaborate tomb in the Valley of the Kings in Egypt. Because of looting, however, his mummy was transferred several times to other places until it was eventually discovered inside an ordinary wooden coffin along with the remains of more than 50 ancient kings, queens and other members of royalty. His remains are now on display in the National Museum of Egyptian Civilization in Cairo, Egypt.[152]

THE WAY OF ALL FLESH

Like Ramesses, the founders and leaders of every religious system in the ancient or modern world died. The grave of the Prophet Muhammad is inside a covered shrine surrounded by two intertwined walls in Medina, Saudi Arabia.[153] Confucius is buried in the Cemetery of Confucius in his hometown of Qufu in Shandong Province, China, along with some of his disciples and many thousands of his descendants.[154] Gautama Buddha's body was cremated in Kushinagar in India. His remains, including his bones, were kept as relics and distributed among various Indian kingdoms.[155]

Jesus Christ also died. However, unlike Ramesses and these other religious leaders, the tomb of Jesus Christ is empty.

Ramesses, Muhammad, Confucius, Buddha and Jesus were all born. They all lived. And they all died. Only Jesus claimed to have risen from the dead. That claim has been challenged repeatedly during the last

2,000 years, but it has withstood the criticism and been embraced by some of the greatest minds of all time, including some who had set out specifically to disprove it.

CAN MIRACLES HAPPEN?

Skeptics often rule out the possibility of Jesus rising from the dead, along with every other miracle recorded in the Bible, on presuppositional grounds. They simply assume that miracles *cannot* happen, and therefore decide not to look at the actual facts in the case.

However, if there really is an all-powerful Being who created the heavens and the earth and all that exists out of nothing, then it certainly wouldn't be particularly difficult or inappropriate for Him to perform what we would consider a miracle at certain key points in history to demonstrate His power and authority over the natural world, to be a sign to validate a special message or messenger, or to reveal an important truth.

There have certainly been many false claims down through the ages where people have been mistaken or deceived into thinking that a miracle had occurred when, in fact, there was none. But that does not invalidate the possibility that true miracles could have occurred at other times and in other places. The question, therefore, should not be, "*Could* God have performed a miracle?" But rather, "*Did* God, in fact, perform one?"

Contrary to what is popularly thought, the ancient world was *not* filled with accounts of the miraculous. Most of the recorded "miracles" that were supposed to have occurred in ancient times were miracles of healing where the sick person had some kind of internal problem or was infertile or had some other ailment that was difficult to test objectively. Or they were done capriciously with outlandish details that clearly place them in the realm of mythological legend. The blind man whose healing is reported in the Gospel of John was correct when he noted, "Nobody has ever heard of opening the eyes of a man born blind."[156]

The miracles recorded in the Bible are of a completely different nature than those recorded in other ancient literature. Some are clearly supernatural events displaying power over nature, such as parting the Red Sea, or walking on water, or feeding more than 5,000 people with five small loaves of bread and two small fish. Others are natural events or heightened natural events with very precise timing, such as the plagues brought on Egypt, or the occurrence of an earthquake that destroyed the people involved in Korah's rebellion. The healing miracles recorded in the Bible are very often external in nature, like restoring a withered hand, or opening the eyes of a man who had been born blind, or bringing back to life a person who had clearly been dead.

And all of them had a definite purpose that was in keeping with the character and purposes of God.

THE MOST IMPORTANT MIRACLE

The Apostle Paul saw the resurrection of Jesus Christ as the cornerstone of Christianity. The truth of whether or not He actually rose from the dead was for Paul the key factor in determining the validity of the Christian faith.

> "...if Christ has not been raised, our preaching is useless and so is your faith. More than that, we are then found to be false witnesses about God, for we have testified about God that He raised Christ from the dead ... if Christ has not been raised, your faith is futile; you are still in your sins ... If only for this life we have hope in Christ, we are to be pitied more than all men."[157]

There were other occurrences recorded in the Bible where someone who had died was brought back to life. The resurrection of Jesus Christ, however, was qualitatively different from those. In each of the other instances, the people were resuscitated. They were brought back to life, but they all eventually died again. Jesus rose from the dead never to die again. In keeping with God's character and purpose, the resurrection demonstrated with power that Jesus was who He said He was, and provided proof to the world that He had completely conquered mankind's greatest enemy – death.

The resurrection of the future Messiah was prophesied in the Old Testament. Isaiah 53:11 records,

"After the suffering of his soul, he will see the light of life and be satisfied."

Psalm 16:9-10 reads,

"Therefore my heart is glad and my tongue rejoices; my body also will rest secure, because you will not abandon me to the grave, nor will you let your Holy One see decay."

Jesus Himself had predicted on several occasions that He would be put to death and then rise again to life.

"Jesus took the Twelve aside and told them, 'We are going up to Jerusalem, and everything that is written by the prophets about the Son of Man will be fulfilled. He will be handed over to the Gentiles. They will mock Him, insult

Him, spit on Him, flog Him and kill Him. On the third day He will rise again.'"[158]

The Gospel writers claim to record eyewitness testimony that Jesus actually died by crucifixion at the hands of the Romans. That His body was prepared for burial and placed in a guarded tomb. And that He miraculously rose from the dead, appeared to several people with whom He spoke and ate, and who He allowed to touch Him to see that He was not some kind of apparition. The apostle Paul summed up the witness of the apostles which he passed on to his readers as of first importance:

> "... that Christ died for our sins according to the Scriptures, that He was buried, that He was raised on the third day according to the Scriptures, and that he appeared to Peter, and then to the Twelve. After that, He appeared to more than five hundred of the brothers at the same time, most of whom are still living ... then He appeared to James, then to all the apostles, and last of all He appeared to me also ..."[159]

WHAT REALLY HAPPENED?

Most of the major Hollywood motion pictures on the

life of Christ treat the resurrection very cautiously. The producers don't seem to know what to do with it. Did it really happen, or didn't it? They usually leave the question somewhat up in the air so no one will be offended. They are generally fairly straightforward when they portray the other miracles that Jesus performed, but when it comes to the resurrection they invariably try to straddle the fence. The guards will be stationed far away from the entrance of the tomb, and Jesus will appear somewhat ethereally to His disciples who gaze at Him with wide eyed amazement as if they were on drugs.

So, what really did happen? Did Jesus rise from the dead or didn't He?

Several theories have been proposed over the centuries to try to explain away the testimony of the apostles. It has been suggested that Jesus didn't die, that the disciples lied and stole the body, that they were in some way deceived, and that the women went to the wrong tomb. Let's look at each of those alternatives.

MAYBE HE DIDN'T DIE!

Several years ago, I had a conversation with an atheist physician who told me he was convinced that Jesus never actually died on the cross. He only passed out, and then woke up in the tomb.

I asked him to think as a physician. Did he believe

it would really be possible for someone who had been brutally beaten and whipped by professional executioners, who had large iron spikes driven through his wrists and ankle joints, had his side pierced through with a spear, was bound up like a mummy in linen wrappings weighed down with 75 pounds of spices, and who was placed on a cold stone slab inside a rock hewn tomb with neither warmth nor food or drink nor medical care to be able to somehow revive, break out of the wrappings, perform the superhuman feat of moving aside a two-ton stone and either overpower or sneak past guards who would have been executed if they had fallen asleep on duty?

Then, if this physician were a disciple who saw someone who had gone through that agonizing procedure appear in front of him gasping for breath and literally appearing half-dead, would he have been encouraged to withstand intense persecution during the rest of his life and die as a martyr so he could experience that quality of a resurrected life. If anything like that ever really happened, the most likely response from anyone looking at the pathetic form in front of them would be, "If that is what rising from the dead is like, let me die and stay dead!"

MAYBE IT WAS A PLOT!

The suggestion that the disciples lied and stole the

body was one of the very first explanations given to explain the empty tomb. When the Jewish chief priests and elders first heard the news of what happened from the guards,

> "... they gave the soldiers a large sum of money, telling them, 'You are to say, "His disciples came during the night and stole him away while we were asleep." If this report gets to the governor, we will satisfy him and keep you out of trouble.'"[160]

This explanation encounters several difficulties. First of all, if it were simply a lie, why didn't someone refute the disciples claim by going to the tomb and producing the dead body? They could have easily proved that the whole thing was a fabrication by simply putting the body on a cart and wheeling it through the center of Jerusalem. The reason they didn't produce the body, of course, is that the body was no longer there.

Second, the disciples experienced tremendous suffering, persecution and ultimately death defending their belief that Jesus did, in fact, rise from the dead. People are not normally willing to suffer and die for a known lie. And the greater the number of people who are involved in a plot, the greater the chances that at least one of them will give in to pressure and conscience, and admit the truth. The fact that none of the disciples or any of the numerous other people who personally saw Jesus alive after the crucifixion and suffered as a result of it admitted that their testimony was false is powerful evidence that they at least believed that what they saw and experienced was true. If the foundation of their entire message were a lie, they would have to be the greatest hypocrites ... and the greatest fools ... who have ever lived.

Third, the suggestion that the disciples lied and stole the body doesn't provide a satisfactory explanation for the phenomenal transformation in their lives. When Jesus was arrested, the disciples ran away in fear. They were dejected, disoriented and dispirited. After the resurrection, there was a boldness and power associated with their witness that amazed even their enemies.

Peter, who had denied even knowing Jesus three times prior to the crucifixion, began speaking with tremendous boldness to the people in Jerusalem after Jesus rose from the dead. On several occasions, he and other disciples were seized by the authorities, beaten, put in jail, and even put to death. When questioned by the high priest and other officials, Peter sharply rebuked them to their face.

Peter, James and almost all of the other disciples of Jesus died martyrs' deaths specifically because of their belief that Jesus had risen from the dead. The only disciple who did not face martyrdom was John, who died in exile on a remote island. After seeing the courage of the disciples, and realizing that they were "unschooled, ordinary men," the authorities were "astonished, and they took note that these men had been with Jesus."[161]

Not only does this explanation not square with what we know of the ethical teaching and lives of the disciples, it also does not fit with what we know of the discipline of Roman soldiers. For a group of untrained, fearful men to have crept passed sleeping guards, moved a two-ton stone and stolen the body without waking the soldiers would seem to defy imagination.

When Jesus' body was placed in the tomb, the tomb was secured by putting a seal on the stone and posting a guard of four soldiers at the entrance. The seal represented the authority of the Roman government and was to be protected at any cost. Roman soldiers were subjected to the severest discipline in the world. The penalty for sleeping on duty was death. As one man has commented, "Those soldiers weren't so tough ... they just conquered the world!"

MAYBE THE DISCIPLES WERE DECEIVED!

Many people who are not comfortable with the idea that the disciples would actually lie suggest that they truly *believed* that Jesus rose from the dead, but they were mistaken. They usually attribute the mistake to some kind of deception or mass hallucination.

Down through history, many people have been deceived into believing that a particular leader was some kind of miracle worker. That Jesus, Himself, was the author of the proposed deception in this case is ruled out by the fact that He was dead. The Jewish authorities certainly did not want the rumor to spread that Jesus had risen from the dead, nor did the Roman governor. Hallucinations occur when people are distraught and want to believe something, but hallucinations occur to individuals, not groups.

The clear witness of the disciples is that they saw Jesus as a group on several occasions after He purportedly rose from the dead. They ate with Him. They touched Him. They talked at length with Him. And they were given "many convincing proofs" that it was actually Jesus who was appearing to them.

Although Jesus had predicted that He would rise from the dead, the disciples had not understood what He meant, nor believed it when the first reports were brought to them. They had been skeptics, and were convinced by the evidence that it was true.

MAYBE THE WOMEN WENT TO THE WRONG TOMB!

One final theory that has been proposed is that the

women who first reported that Jesus had risen from the dead actually went to the wrong tomb. They were sad, emotional and simply made an honest mistake. Since they had hoped that what they had experienced watching Jesus being crucified was all a nightmare, they were overjoyed when they saw an empty tomb, and rushed to report that Jesus had risen.

While that explanation may seem plausible at first, it doesn't bear up under closer scrutiny. Since the women had previously seen the tomb where the body of Jesus had been placed and there was a Roman guard surrounding the entrance to the tomb, it would be highly unlikely that they would have gone to the wrong place on that fateful Sunday morning. It's even more unlikely that the disciples who went to check up on the women's statement would also have gone to the wrong tomb, not to mention the Jewish authorities who asked for a Roman guard to be stationed at the tomb to prevent the body from being stolen.

And, then, of course, there were the Roman guards who were stationed at the *right* tomb!

MAYBE HE ACTUALLY ROSE!

In 1930, a British advertising agent and freelance writer by the name of Albert Henry Ross and writing under the pseudonym Frank Morison, published the results of a personal study he undertook to discover the underlying, non-miraculous "truth" behind the crucifixion and resurrection of Jesus. He was an honest inquirer who took great pains to look very carefully at the available evidence.

He wrote the book, but to his great surprise, it turned out to be a classic work *defending* the resurrection of Christ, not debunking it![162]

He wrote in *Who Moved the Stone?* for all of his readers to ponder:

> "This study is in some ways so unusual and provocative that the writer thinks it desirable to state here very briefly how the book came to take its present form.

> "In one sense it could have taken no other, for it is essentially a confession, the inner story of a man who originally set out to write one kind of book and found himself compelled by the sheer force of circumstances to write quite another.

> "It is not that the facts themselves altered, for they are recorded imperishably in the monuments and in the pages of human history. But the interpretation to be put upon the facts underwent a change. Somehow the perspective shifted – not suddenly, as in a flash of insight

or inspiration, but slowly, almost imperceptibly, by the very stubbornness of the facts themselves.

"The book as it was originally planned was left high and dry ...

"There may be, and, as the writer thinks, there certainly is, a deep and profoundly historical basis for that much disputed sentence in the Apostles' Creed – 'The *third day* he rose again from the dead.'"[163]

10

WHAT ABOUT THIS THING CALLED PAIN?

"Have you considered My servant Job?"

That question, posed by God to Satan, is from a book that is recognized as one of the greatest poetic masterpieces of all time on the subject of suffering – the Book of Job in the Bible.[164]

The main character, Job, was the greatest man among all the people of the East. He was materially successful and greatly respected by all who knew him. In the Prologue to the book, God Himself said of Job that there was no one on earth like him. He was blameless and upright, a man who feared God and shunned evil.[165] And yet, Satan takes away all of Job's material goods – including the lives of his seven children – and then afflicts him with painful sores from the soles of his feet to the top of his head.

The main body of the book is a debate between Job and three of his friends who have come to offer him counsel. When they first see him, they are appalled by what they see. They weep aloud, tear their robes, sprinkle dust on their heads and sit on the ground with him for seven days without saying a word because of the depth of his suffering. Then they begin to share with him, one by one, what they believe is the cause of this intense pain and anguish.

Their conclusion? Job must have committed very grave personal sin. He must be a truly wicked man because God would never allow an innocent person to experience such extreme misery. They urge him to acknowledge the extent of what he has done wrong, seek forgiveness and then they are sure that Job will experience the blessing of God.

Job's response is that he hasn't done anything remotely worthy of such severe punishment, and he can't understand why he is being subjected to such excessive suffering.

Throughout the book, neither Job nor his counselors are aware of the real reason for Job's suffering. Not only did God *allow* Satan to take away all his possessions and afflict his body with painful sores, God actually *initiated* the discussion with Satan that led to the calamities.

And that brings up the real issue of the Book of Job, and an issue that philosophers, theologians and normal, everyday people have wrestled with since the beginning of time:

"Why would a good and all-powerful God allow the righteous to suffer and the wicked to prosper?"

THE PROBLEM OF PAIN

One of the most often presented challenges to a belief in God, and one that has been the determining factor for many people who have lost their childhood faith, relates to the existence of pain and suffering in the world. The reasoning is clear. If God were *good*, He would not want excessive pain and suffering to exist. If He were *all-powerful*, He would have prevented excessive pain and suffering from happening. Since excessive pain and suffering exist in the world, God must not be all-powerful, or He must not be good!

An additional problem for those who believe that the Bible really is God's Word is that the Bible records God Himself as commanding His people to utterly destroy every man, woman and child when He sent them against certain of their enemies.

"... in the cities of the nations the LORD your God is giving you as an inheritance, do not leave alive anything that breathes. Completely destroy them – the Hittites, Amorites, Canaanites, Perizzites, Hivites and Jebusites – as the LORD your God has commanded you."[166]

How could a God like that be good? He not only allows pain and suffering to exist in the world, He even commands that people, including innocent children, be killed! Does God enjoy watching people suffer and die?

PAIN IS CERTAINLY REAL!

Everyone in this world experiences pain to one degree or another. In and of itself, that is not a bad thing. In fact, it's a necessary good for life in the world in which we live. Much like a warning light on a car dashboard, pain alerts us to real or potential danger. There is actually a disease which is compounded by the fact that its sufferers do not feel pain in their extremities. The disease is leprosy. Because they do not feel pain, lepers do not realize when they have stubbed a toe or cut themselves or picked up a hot item. As a result, they gradually see their extremities become hideously marred.

Some pain comes from physical suffering, ranging from a mild headache ... to the intense pain a woman experiences in labor when giving birth to a child ... to the chronic pain that often accompanies trauma or the late stages of cancer. There is also the pain that comes from emotional distress, resulting from anxiety or shame or sorrow. In many cases, the physical pain in a given situation is manageable, but the accompanying emotional distress of seeing little or no purpose in it is overwhelming.

And then there is the pain that comes from difficult circumstances in life. The psychological difficulties of living as a paraplegic or as someone with a severe handicap, for example, is an underlying reason why many people strongly favor aborting unborn children or euthanizing those who are in what they would consider an unbearably difficult situation. Finally, there is the pain that results from reckless behavior and man's inhumanity to man. The emotional distress of a mother whose only child has been killed by a drunk driver, or the physical and psychological pain experienced by tortured prisoners of war legitimately prompt the question, "Why would God ever allow that to happen?"

After all, they shoot horses, don't they? If we are compassionate to animals that are suffering, why is God not compassionate to people who are suffering? Isn't He being cruel to allow people to live in pain and hopelessness without doing something to alleviate it?

HOW MUCH IS TOO MUCH?

Part of the answer to the question, "Why is there excessive pain and suffering in the world?" depends, of course, on how the word "excessive" is defined. For some, the slightest physical pain or emotional distress is excessive. For others, a great deal of pain and distress can be tolerated, and even be seen as a vital part of accomplishing some greater end. Athletes often share the sentiment, "No pain. No gain."

Nevertheless, great pain and suffering does exist in this world, and it is often experienced by those who did nothing to deserve it!

Consider, for example, the case of a terminally ill patient, Diane. Her story was reported in the *New England Journal of Medicine.*

"Diane was a fifty-year old woman who refused treatment for leukemia. (The treatment is rigorous and painful and offers only 25 percent chance of recovery.) She told the physician that she had gotten information on suicide from the Hemlock Society ... The doctor says, 'It was extraordinarily important to Diane to maintain control of herself and her own dignity during the time remaining to her. When this was no longer possible, she clearly wanted to die.'

"The doctor was convinced that she would not take her life until the disease reached the point at which 'bone pain, weakness, fatigue, and fevers' began to dominate. He also believed that 'the security of having enough barbiturates available to commit suicide when and if the time came would leave her secure enough to live fully and concentrate on the present ... 'I wrote the prescription with an uneasy feeling about the boundaries I was exploring...

"She reached the point 'she feared the most – increasing discomfort, dependence, and hard choices between pain and sedation.' She said her final good-byes to her husband and college age son, asked them to leave for an hour, and ended her life. The doctor reports, 'I called the medical examiner to inform him that a hospice patient had died. When asked about the cause of death, I said, "acute leukemia" ... Although I know we have measures to help control pain and lessen suffering, to think that people do not suffer in the process of dying is an illusion. Prolonged dying can occasionally be peaceful, but more often the role of the physician and family is limited to lessening but not eliminating severe suffering.'"[167]

Diane certainly came to the conclusion that the pain and suffering she was experiencing was "excessive," to the point that she decided to take her own life. Why didn't God "do something" about it!?

A DIVING ACCIDENT

How about the case of a depressed teenager who became a quadriplegic as a result of a diving accident? Joni Eareckson wrote after the accident,

"To Whom It May Concern:

"I hate my life. You can't imagine the ache of wanting to end your life and not being able to because you're a quadriplegic and can't use your hands.

"After the doctors did surgery on my neck, I refused to wear a neck collar. I hate it, too. Nobody understands and nobody will listen to me when I tell them I don't want to live. People feel sorry for me and I can't stand it. I can't even go to the bathroom by myself.

"I don't have the energy to cope. I don't have the strength to face the next day. I want out."[168]

Because of the emotional anguish she was experiencing, Joni wanted to take her own life, but could not because of her completely debilitating injury. If God is real, and if He is good, why doesn't He do something to alleviate that kind of suffering?

BIRTH DEFECTS

What about the situation of Lori and Reba Schappell, conjoined twins born in 1961 whose story was reported in *The New York Times*?[169]

Conjoined twins, or what are commonly called "Siamese Twins," occur in about 1 in 50,000 – 100,000 births. Some are attached only by pieces of skin tissue and can easily be separated by a surgical procedure. Some, however, share vital organs which make it impossible to separate them without killing one or both.

In this case, the girls are joined at the head, with portions of their skull, scalp and blood vessels fused at the side in a mirror-image configuration so that they actually face in opposite directions. When one is facing forward, the other is facing backward. One of the sisters is also significantly shorter than the other, so they are unable to walk together. Because of how they are joined, it is impossible to separate the two without killing them both. Where one goes, the other goes. There is no way to "get alone" because they are physically attached to one another.

Because of the availability of ultrasound and other fetal diagnostic procedures, an increasing number of conjoined twins are being aborted because people cannot imagine living in such a "horrible" condition. If God is real, all-powerful, and good, why would He not do something to prevent that kind of terrible situation to occur? There is no connection between the behavior of the parents and the occurrences of these and many other birth defects.

Why doesn't God put an end to such "innocent" suffering?

TORTURE

Perhaps the most "excessive" pain and suffering experienced by people is the physical and psychological pain experienced by victims of torture, because the pain is purposely inflicted with the specific intent of making it impossible to bear. Eugene B. McDaniel, a captured US Navy pilot who spent years in a prison camp in North Vietnam, is just one of many examples throughout history of people who have been tortured:

"... they put me into the ropes, a treatment I was to know and dread in the long pull ahead. They tied my wrists tight, then pulled my arms high behind me, binding me so that my shoulder bones were ready to pop ... I pretended to pass out several times in hopes they would untie me and leave me alone. But they were wise to that. At times I would bite my shoulder hard to try to transfer the pain from one area to another. Then I began pounding my head against the wall, hoping for blood, something liquid to ease my terrible thirst ...

"I knew I was up against a monstrous situation, against an enemy who seemed to take great satisfaction in inflicting pain, who performed like robots in doing so. The question I had to face now was: Could I take that kind of torture again? And, of course, the other question: Was it so important that I refuse to answer their questions anyway? In the hours and days ahead, I was to feel this nagging question even more strongly as I listened to the screams of my fellow pilots going through the same torture, some maybe even worse. I had more coming too. I knew it."[170]

Why would God allow people to torture other people? Couldn't He have prevented it in some way?

FREE TO CHOOSE

If God is real, and He is *all-powerful*, then it necessarily follows that whatever level of pain and suffering exists in the world must have been permitted or intended by Him, and must be part of His overall plan for life and existence. If He is real, and also *good*, then the level of pain and suffering that He allows or commands must have some positive purpose.

Much of the pain in this world that is considered excessive is the direct result of what has historically been called "sinful" or "evil" behavior. Those terms can be defined in various ways, of course, depending on a person's philosophical or religious outlook. However, although people differ widely on what they consider evil, all agree that some things are clearly right and some things are clearly wrong. Atrocities in war, child abuse, and murdering or maiming innocent people all result in pain and suffering, and are all the result of people consciously or unconsciously hurting others ... which brings us to an underlying issue that needs to be addressed before we look specifically at the problem of pain:

"Why would a good God allow evil to exist in His creation. If He were God, and good, couldn't He have made everyone good?"

The answer to that question is actually, "No!"

Because He is God, and because He is good, He has chosen to give mankind a *true* freewill. God could have made us all like computerized automatons who always did His bidding. When asked, "Do you love Me?" we would be programmed to respond with, "Yes ... passionately!" Even if it were possible to program the response to be emotionally intense, the response would still be hollow and fake. It would not have been given freely.

Inherent in God's decision to give mankind a true

freewill is the potential for mankind to say, "No! I don't want to do things Your way! I want to do them *my* way!"

WHERE DID PAIN AND SUFFERING COME FROM?

Because God is infinite and omniscient, He knows all of the relevant factors in every situation. We, on the other hand, are finite and limited in our understanding, and can only be aware of some of the relevant factors. As mentioned earlier, the Biblical teaching on the subject is that pain and suffering entered the world in the Garden of Eden when the first man and woman freely chose to disobey God and eat the forbidden fruit.

God permitted pain, suffering and death to enter His creation because it was, ultimately, in our best interests to be free to choose. He did not, however, abandon mankind when they rejected His offer of life and peace. Incorporated in God's plan was a way for Adam and Eve and their descendants to regain the paradise that had been lost. That is the unfolding message of the Bible.

However, while the Biblical teaching on the origin of pain and suffering, and the hidden purposes of God may be true and may sound great, that doesn't minimize the intensity of the pain and suffering that people actually feel in the real world. Regardless of where pain came from, and how, when, and why it entered the world, isn't God still being cruel by allowing excessive pain to exist?

Or ... is God able to actually use the pain and suffering He allows to exist to accomplish good purposes in the world, and in the lives of the people who experience it?

11

WHY WOULD GOD ALLOW PAIN TO EXIST?

*"Why are you using your ignorance
to deny My providence?"[171]*

Throughout the debate in the book of Job, Job and his three counselors assume that it is God who has brought about Job's suffering, and that the suffering is some sort of punishment. The counselors are convinced that Job's sins must be great because his suffering is great. But Job knows that he is not a grave sinner and assumes that God is punishing him unjustly.

Then, a young man shows up. He explains that he had waited for his elders to speak first, but finally could not hold back his concerns. He tells both Job and Job's friends that they have misunderstood what was happening. The older men have failed to prove that Job is a wicked man who deserves to be punished. And Job has been too quick to speak and judge God for wrongly punishing him without waiting for God to provide an answer to his dilemma.

That is when God Himself speaks to Job out of a whirlwind.

He asks him a long series of questions to contrast His infinite knowledge and understanding of the creation and life to Job's finite ability to fully grasp what God is doing in the world. Through this questioning, God makes it increasingly clear that He knows things that we don't know, and He has worthy purposes for the things He allows to happen that we may be completely unaware of.

In Job's case, neither he nor his friends knew anything about the most significant factor related to his misfortunes – the conversations that God had with Satan prior to Job's trials. God was not *testing* Job to see if he was strong enough to be used in God's service, nor was He *punishing* Job for things he had done wrong. Rather, God knew the depth of Job's character and was actually *employing* him in His service. He was showing how a true person of integrity responds to difficult trials.

At the end of the book, we learn that God restored Job's fortune with double the amount of material goods he had before. He was given twice as many sheep, camels, yoke of oxen and donkeys. Interestingly, he was only given the same number of children. Why? Because one day Job would again be reunited with his original children in heaven.

But the suffering of Job also resulted in other positive benefits in his life. After God speaks to him, Job explains,

> "I have declared that which I did not understand, things too wonderful for me, which I did not know ... I have heard of You by the hearing of the ear; but now my eye sees You"[172]

God used the tragic events that Job went through to bring him into a significantly closer and deeper relationship with Him. Job also had the personal satisfaction of knowing that he had successfully accomplished the task to which God had called him. Satan was shown that he was wrong in his assessment of how an upright man would respond to tragedy. And the record of what happened has provided important insights for later generations of people, including us, into better understanding God and His ways.

In the end, the book doesn't provide a comprehensive list of reasons for why God allows good people to suffer bad things. God ultimately has many reasons that are beyond our limited ability to understand. But He does answer Job, and the answer He gives is the only sufficient answer that could be given in light of who we are as finite human beings. The ultimate answer of the book of Job is that the God of heaven is trustworthy and will never abandon those who seek Him. He had a worthy purpose for Job's suffering, and He revealed Himself to Job at the proper time.

Does God have worthy purposes for the suffering He permits in *our* lives?

AN ESSENTIAL QUALITY OF LIFE

The Bible mentions a specific quality that it considers to be priceless. It's more profitable than gold or silver. It's more precious than jewels. It leads to long life, happiness, honor and peace. And nothing you or I desire compares with it. That quality is *wisdom*.[173]

Wisdom is looking at life from God's perspective because He sees things as they really are. He is not limited and sees the big picture. He sees the long term, not just the short term. He alone is able to take all factors into consideration in a given situation, not just some.

An important part of wisdom as we look at why God would allow pain and suffering to exist is the ability to look beneath the surface of a matter to see important facts and relationships that others often miss.

IS THERE A "BOTTOM LINE" TO PAIN?

God has set an upper limit to the level of pain any person will ever experience.

There is an upper threshold of pain, beyond which

our bodies naturally shut down, either when the specific area of pain goes numb, or the entire body goes unconscious. What that means, in practical terms, is that we will never experience truly *unbearable* pain. That upper level is definitely intense, and we often don't like the boundaries that God has set, thinking they are much too wide. But the truth is that God has set definite limits on the level of pain that any one person will ever experience, in accordance with His wisdom and grace.

After describing the severe pain and suffering he went through with his first experience as a victim of torture, Captain McDaniels came to a rather surprising conclusion:

> "Yet I had taken the first round of agony without telling them anything they really wanted. Something had risen to the surface in me, some quality of resistance. From where? Was it my old athletic discipline? Was it the military code I had followed for the past twelve years – the pride in sticking to it, no matter what? Was it my fragile faith in God? Maybe. I had to admit right then, however, that my faith in God had taken a nosedive back in the jungle when those Jolly Greens didn't show up and the Vietnamese home guard did instead. I really

didn't know what faith I had that was strong enough to hold me in the future.

"But I kept coming back to the big point: I *had* come through a very bad time, my initial baptism in torture. I had been shaken to the depths of my emotional and physical makeup. My mind was drained, and I had a hard time focusing on any given thought pattern for long. *Yet I had come through.*"[174]

The body's ability to withstand severe pain is a fascinating subject that is still not completely understood. Dr. Jack van Hoff, MD was a friend and Associate Professor of Pediatrics, Hematology/Oncology at the Yale University School of Medicine when I talked with him about this subject. As a physician who specializes in treating children with cancer, he is well acquainted with the effects of pain, as well as the need for pain management.

"Pain is a very complex phenomenon. There is clearly an upper threshold of pain, beyond which a person is first incapacitated and then even becomes unconscious. However, that threshold can change dramatically, depending on the state of mind and physical circumstances of the person experiencing it.

"There have been many examples of soldiers, political prisoners, prisoners of war, and even ordinary individuals not particularly insensitive to pain under normal circumstances, who were actually able to withstand tremendous pain and distress from wounds or torture when the circumstances required it.

"It's a phenomenon the medical and scientific communities have studied, but still do not fully understand."[175]

Not everyone who experiences torture is able to say with Captain McDaniels that they were able to come through it alive, and, in one sense, strengthened as a result. Many have, in fact, actually died in the process. Many, including Captain McDaniels, withstood for a time, gave in but were not broken, and were subjected to it again. For many, the pain itself was not as intense as the anticipation of it. But the clear fact of the matter is that God has placed within our bodies mechanisms that actually help manage pain to the extent that even victims of torture have been able to withstand it.

WHAT ELSE IS THERE?

God has also given mankind medications that are very effective in relieving pain, along with caring people who provide tremendous help in lessening the difficulties of going through suffering.

The Dana-Farber Cancer Institute conducted an extensive survey on people's views of how "excessive" excessive pain really is. What they found was that, while many patients and the general public generally think they'd rather be dead than live with severe pain before they are actually in that situation, once confronted personally with pain and terminal illness, their views change.

> "People may look at a terminally ill patient and think, 'I'd rather die than be like that.' But, our data indicate that what cancer patients with pain are really interested in is getting rid of pain, not in dying."[176]

The reason why we "shoot horses" is because we don't want to spend the money or put forth the effort to care for them.

Controlling pain is highly advanced. There is pain, and it is real. But God has designed life in such a way that there is not only an upper limit on the amount of pain and suffering people will experience, but medications, along with friends, relatives and compassionate people in special medical centers, all help to make pain manageable ... which brings us to the all important question that everyone wants to know the answer to.

WHY?

God has purposes for suffering, and those purposes are good.

If you were to ask yourself or almost anyone who has experienced personal pain and suffering to one degree or another what benefit the experience produced, you would probably get a variety of answers. That's because God actually has many good purposes for why He allows pain and suffering to occur.

CHARACTER DEVELOPMENT

One answer that many people give is that the pain and suffering were instrumental in *developing character*. Many of life's greatest lessons are learned directly as a result of being forced to confront some unpleasant circumstance.

That truth vividly impacted me many years ago through the life of a man I knew only as Dr. Brewster. He was paralyzed and in a wheelchair, taken from place to place on the grounds of the organization I was working with at the time by a kind woman. He sometimes wore what I thought were rather strange outfits, but he seemed to speak quite pleasantly to the various people who came up to him. I never had occasion to actually talk with him myself, but I looked at him from a distance and felt sorry for him.

To my surprise one day, he was the featured

speaker at a special event at work where he told the staff about his early life as a competition diver. He explained that he had become paralyzed as a result of a diving accident. And then, he made the most amazing statement I had ever heard. He said that *the diving accident was the most significant, positive event of his life!* Why? Because that event refocused his life from pursuing what was trivial to pursuing what was significant!

Dr. Brewster went on to tell how he and his wife, the woman who always pushed his wheelchair and who was also a Dr. Brewster, had the privilege of traveling all over the world to consult with missionary organizations, businesses and governments on linguistic matters. Had it not been for his diving accident, he would have frittered away his life pursuing self-centered, trivial goals. Instead, he and his wife were two of the top linguists in the world. Some of the "strange" things I had noted about his wardrobe were personal gifts given to him by leaders and heads-of-state in other lands.

The apostle Paul had personally experienced a great deal of pain, deprivation, and even torture. In one of his letters recorded in the New Testament he gave his credentials. He had been

"... in prison more frequently, been flogged

more severely, and been exposed to death again and again. Five times I received from the Jews the forty lashes minus one. Three times I was beaten with rods, once I was stoned, three times I was shipwrecked, I spent a night and a day in the open sea. I have been constantly on the move. I have been in danger from rivers, in danger from bandits, in danger from my own countrymen, in danger from Gentiles; in danger in the city, in danger in the country, in danger at sea; and in danger from false brothers. I have labored and toiled and have often gone without sleep. I have known hunger and thirst and have often gone without food; I have been cold and naked."[177]

Did he believe that God had abandoned him in all this? On the contrary, he knew that God had good purposes for it all. He explained it this way to his readers:

"...we also rejoice in our sufferings, because we know that suffering produces perseverance; perseverance, character; and character, hope. And hope does not disappoint us because God has poured out His love into our hearts by the Holy Spirit, whom He has given us."[178]

Developing character is a primary reason why God allows painful trials to come into our lives.

PROVIDE DIRECTION

Another one of God's good purposes for suffering is to *provide direction.*

Limitations do not prevent us from doing things that are truly worthwhile and significant. Rather, they define the sphere in which those things can be done, and often empower us to do them more effectively.

I first learned that lesson personally from a young man I was interviewing for a possible position with an organization I was working with. The position he was applying for would require him to speak before groups of people. He was crippled in his legs and had to wear braces to stand. I asked him if he would feel somewhat self-conscious standing before a group of people to address them in that condition. To my complete surprise and encouragement, he responded by saying that he would actually look forward to it. He likened his condition to that of an artillery division in a battle. He was not as mobile as the infantry, he said, but, when he struck, it was with a great deal more power.

I saw the truth of that in action a couple of years later. I was in a singing group that had as part of its program an opportunity for some of the group members to share from their personal experience how God had worked in their lives. The audiences were always pleasant and would listen politely to each of the members who had something to say.

When one young woman stepped up to the microphone, however, there was a hush throughout the auditorium and everyone listened intently as she told her story. She was attractive, but usually wore long skirts because as a child her leg had to be amputated. As she explained how she learned of God's love through that painful experience, she touched people's hearts much more deeply than any of the others in the group.

Joni Eareckson Tada, the teenage athlete who was left a quadriplegic as a result of an accident and wrote that she hated life and wanted to die, has since become an internationally known speaker and author, and the founder of an organization that is an aggressive advocate for the handicapped. Because of her own severe handicap, she is able to speak with great authority on the grace of God and the purposes He has for suffering.

The suffering that each of these people went through did not prevent them from experiencing a full and meaningful life. Rather, it defined the direction their lives would take.

DEMONSTRATE GOD'S POWER AND GRACE

A third purpose that God has for allowing suffering to exist in His creation is to provide occasions for God to *demonstrate His power and grace.*

God actually demonstrates His power in the lives of people going through suffering in two very different ways. On many occasions, He delivers them from the situation that is causing the pain and distress. At other times, He allows them to remain in the situation, and provides the inner strength to bear the burden. Sometimes, He will provide the strength to bear up under the burden for a while, and then bring deliverance.

While the lives of Lori and Reba Schappell, the conjoined twins mentioned earlier, seem unbearably difficult for most of us to imagine, they don't see it that way. God has given them the grace to not only bear up under it, but to also delight in their situation.

"There are good days and bad days – so what? ... This is what we know. We don't hate it. We live it every day. I don't sit around questioning it, or asking myself what I could do differently if I were separated."[179]

Reba is short and unable to walk for herself, so her sister wheels her around on a bar stool. When asked if they would ever consider going through a surgical operation to separate themselves from one another, their response was,

> "Our point of view is no, straight-out no. Why would you want to do that? For all the money in China, why? You'd be ruining two lives in the process."

In 1997 the sisters flew to California to accept an LA Music Award that Reba won for best new country music artist of the year.[180]

Captain McDaniels experienced God's grace in a fascinating way as he was finally being released from his confinement as a prisoner of war:

> "But looking at Spot [the prison commander] now, I did not feel like gloating ... I knew I had come a long way from my first terrifying moment in that shoot-down. I had come six years in time; but in it, God had turned me around 360 degrees, so that I could stand there and look into the face of a man who had done all he could to break me and yet feel only a desire to share with him the inner, deeper secrets of God and His love and His never-ending care.[181]

When asked by reporters on his release from the prison camp if he felt bitterness toward his captors, he replied,

"No, I had no bitterness at all. So I simply told them that. Maybe it surprised some of the press – maybe it even disappointed some. But I didn't know how to explain that when a man finds God in the deepest point of darkness and comes out not even bitter at the enemy, the question hardly fits."[182]

CHOICES HAVE CONSEQUENCES

Some pain and suffering results from the *natural consequences* of actions or behavior that turns away from God's revealed will and standards.

We don't like to talk about sin in our day, but it's clearly the case that much of the personal pain and suffering that people experience is the direct result of wrong choices those people consciously make.

The famous story of the Prodigal Son in the Bible is an excellent example. Jesus told this parable of a young man who chose to take his family inheritance early in order to leave home, establish his life on his own, and squander his wealth in riotous living. As a result of his foolish choices, he ended up in poverty, feeding pigs and wishing that he would be allowed to eat the food that the pigs were eating.

Finally, the pain that resulted from the natural consequences of his lifestyle choices brought him to his senses. He decided to return to his father to ask if he could become a hired hand on his father's estate. To his great surprise, his father welcomed him back with a display of great love and affection. He had squandered his wealth, however, and nothing he could do could get it back.

I once asked a physician who was head surgeon at a large hospital if he thought lifestyle considerations had a direct impact on hospitalization. His immediate response was, "If people would stop doing three things, you'd get rid of about 70% of hospital visits!"

He went on to explain that, in his experience, about 20% of hospital visits were the result of overeating, an additional 20% resulted from smoking too much, and a third 20% were the result of excessive drinking of alcoholic beverages. Another 10% came from trauma, which he said almost always involved alcohol or drugs.

Those numbers were not arrived at scientifically, but his point was clear. Wrong choices have painful consequences.

HELP OTHERS

God uses pain and suffering in one person's life to significantly *impact the lives of others*.

Many of God's purposes actually extend far beyond an individual person's life to touch the lives of others within their personal web of relationships. It's not unusual for a tragic situation or a person's untimely death to cause others around them to rethink their priorities in life.

Historically, major tragedies have resulted in individuals or a society at large making important decisions. For example, the severe persecution of first century Christians greatly impacted the Roman Empire. As people saw others willing to suffer and die for their faith, many former persecutors became believers, and many timid believers were emboldened to speak out courageously. The apostle Paul wrote from prison to his friends in the city of Philippi,

> "Now I want you to know, brothers, that what has happened to me has really served to advance the gospel. As a result, it has become clear throughout the whole palace guard and to everyone else that I am in chains for Christ. Because of my chains, most of the brothers in the Lord have been encouraged to speak the word of God more courageously and fearlessly."[183]

One personal friend of mine who has a special needs child elegantly expressed how the experience touched her life.

> "My life with my five year old son Daniel has led me to places I never dreamed I would go,

but I have learned after these years of watching Daniel grow, educating myself, learning, investing in his potential, and advocating for his needs, that it is not time that heals, but our growth through experiences. I am proud of his tremendous motivation and the extraordinary gift of having him in my life.

"Before Daniel was born, our lifestyle would have seemed the most remote and unlikely scenario I could have imagined. I was a career woman and I had every reason to assume that after our son was born we would learn about parenting together and eventually I would return to my work and with the help of our Nanny, continue to live the two income life we had planned on. Every assumption I had ever made and every fantasy I had dreamed was shattered within the first 48 hours of Daniel's life when it was made clear to us that all was not 'normal'. … There was no official diagnosis, but we were forewarned that Daniel's future development was at risk …

"Daniel is now 5 yrs. old. I sometimes look at his baby pictures and realize just how far we have come … The prestigious office address and the career I once had are gone for now, and I may never know what it is to have a child who is not challenged, but I have the gifts that Daniel has given me: my memories of his first steps, his first sentence, his irresistible laughter, his contagious spirit, his love of swinging as high as the sky …

"I will always have the memories of our times together at the playground, of holding Daniel close to me, and whispering to him, 'I love you, more that the sun and the moon and the stars.' I want him to know how much he has given me, and often, as we walk home, hand in hand, I sing, 'You are my sunshine, my only sunshine' … It's his favorite song."[184]

The difficulties relating to Daniel's life are used by God to not only work in his life, but, through him, to impact the lives of others in very positive ways.

DEATH AND ETERNITY

There is one, final purpose of God that should be mentioned. Pain and suffering are used by Him as a means of bringing people into His eternal presence.

Death is an aspect of life that every person at some point has to confront. And it's especially important when asking why God would destroy the entire world, as in the Noah's day, or command His people to completely destroy everyone living in certain cities in the land of Canaan – including innocent women and children.

The first thing we should keep in mind as we look at this is that *all life on earth eventually dies.* The question is not "if" a person will die. It is "how and when." As the Creator and righteous Judge of all the earth, God has the authority to give and take life, and the wisdom to know when and how death should and will come.

Second, it's important to understand that evil actions and behavior not only result in pain and suffering to one degree or another in the present, they also result in *increased pain and suffering to future generations.*

God has not only placed a limit on the level of pain and suffering that He will allow any one person to experience, He has also placed a limit on the level of pain and suffering that He will allow any one culture to experience or inflict. The clear lessons from history are that torturous regimes always come to an end, and morally corrupt cultures either disintegrate or are destroyed.

The Flood of Noah's day came as God's judgment on an earth that was filled with wickedness.

"The LORD saw how great man's wickedness on the earth had become, and that every inclination of the thoughts of his heart was only evil all the time. The LORD was grieved that he had made man on the earth, and his heart was filled with pain. So the LORD said, 'I will wipe mankind, whom I have created, from the face of the earth...'"[185]

God said He would spare the city of Sodom if only 10 righteous men could be found in it. They could not, and the cities of Sodom and Gomorrah were destroyed.

God told Abraham that He would not bring an end to the corrupt Canaanite civilization in his day because "the sin of the Amorites has not yet reached its full measure." The judgment came over 400 years later when the level of moral corruption had reached the limit God had set. Because of the decadent lifestyle of its people, venereal disease and other communicable diseases were rampant. To protect innocent people in that generation and in future generations from the ravages of disease and the other effects of their moral decadence, the cities and their contents had to be burned, and that culture had to come to an end.

Third, death is the means by which God brings *an ultimate end* to the pain and suffering of this world, and opens the opportunity for people to experience the blessings that God originally intended for mankind.

Death is not actually a necessary consequence to life. Rather, it is a condition instituted by a good Creator after mankind turned its back on God to prevent His creatures from being forever bound in a state in which they must experience the oppression of their own evil attitudes and actions, and the evil attitudes and actions of others.

Death ultimately provides the way for mankind to regain paradise.

The prophet Isaiah commented,

"The righteous perish, and no one takes it to heart; the devout are taken away, and no one understands that the righteous are taken away to be spared from evil. Those who walk uprightly enter into peace; they find rest as they lie in death."[186]

Jesus told His disciples just before His crucifixion,

"In my Father's house are many mansions: if it were not so, I would have told you. I go to prepare a place for you."[187]

Heaven and hell are issues that are beyond the scope of this book. But let me simply point out here that a prominent belief in the Early Christian Church, and according to some scholars the dominant belief, was that God would ultimately restore *all* of His creation to its intended perfection. They believed that hell is real, but it doesn't last forever. Its purpose is to restore not just to punish. You can read more about this in my book, *Heaven's Doors ... Wider Than You Ever Believed!*[188] It was awarded the Silver Medal in Theology in the Illumination Book Awards for exemplary Christian literature.

THE LAST WORD

Because we are finite creatures with a very limited ability to understand infinite things, we will never fully understand all of God's purposes in any area. We're like a group of toddlers who haven't yet grasped the fact that two plus two equals four, trying to figure out the subtle mathematical complexities of Einstein's General Theory of Relativity. We should try to learn the answers to perplexing questions of life as best we can. However, the ultimate answer to many of our questions is actually found by looking at who God is.

Howard Rutledge was a prisoner of war in North Vietnam for seven years, five of which were spent in solitary confinement. During his time as a POW, he experienced cruel torture, deprivation, and suffering that seemed almost impossible to bear. But he made it through and wrote a book about his experiences. In it, he reflected on his time in the prison the POWs had nicknamed, "Alcatraz."

"I remember Alcatraz as a time of loneliness and misery, constant harassment, torture, and interrogation, but I don't remember one of the Alcatraz Gang ever losing faith in God ... In prison I firmly believed that there was a God who loved me and was working in my life. I cannot explain with reason or proof why my faith was central to my survival. But it was."[189]

God is good. God is wise. He alone is infinite. At the end of time, when all of the factors in any given case are brought to light, we will clearly know that God is real, and be impressed with, and stand in awe of the phenomenal wisdom of the decisions that He has made.

That is really what faith is all about. It is faith in who God is.

EPILOGUE

EXPERIENCING GOD

"George, your background seems to be similar to mine. Would you like to come over tomorrow night for some popcorn and talk?"

t was the Spring of my junior year of college and I had been invited to a meeting of some "Christians" one evening by a young woman who I was hoping to get to know better. When the meeting was over, a young man I had never met named Conrad came up to me and asked that question. I was about to say "no," when I heard my mouth say "sure, what time?"[190]

That night changed my life.

Throughout this book, I've presented information that has convinced me that there is a God who is real, all-powerful and good. He created the heavens and the earth and all that is in them, and left a record of who He is and what He has done in a document we know as the Bible. But knowing *about* God is not the same as *knowing* Him. God is not a distant Being. He desires to have a personal relationship with each person He created in His image.

In my case, I grew up trying to be a good person, but I didn't really have strong convictions about anything and I lacked the inner strength to stand behind the convictions I did have. It was during the Vietnam War era, and I was fearful about the future. I lacked self-discipline. I was doing fairly well in my studies, but the world and life were like a jigsaw puzzle to me. I didn't really see how things fit together, and there was no clear picture to guide me.

I thought there was probably a God, but I couldn't quite figure out how He fit into things. Was He a Santa Claus who gave you good things when you made out a list and checked it twice, keeping in mind that He might be concerned with whether or not you were naughty or nice?

Was He a Divine Watchmaker who put the original universe and life together, started it up, and then left it to run on its own?

Was He like Aladdin's Genie – awesome power in a tiny little living space – at your command if you just rubbed the lamp the right way?

I couldn't quite figure out where Jesus fit into the puzzle, either. Was He a good man? Was He God? I didn't know.

The students I met that night in college, along with Conrad who invited me over for popcorn, seemed to have a different quality of life than I had. They were excited about the future. They were enthusiastic about life. They had a strict set of moral standards, but they seemed to have the inner strength to live up to them.

As we ate popcorn and talked, Conrad shared a simple truth that opened my eyes to what was missing in my understanding of life and God's relationship to it. It was the fact that God was the Creator, and I was the creature. He was active in people's lives not as a servant who did their bidding, but as the Lord who directed and empowered them to do His will. He had a unique plan for each person's life, and He provided power for living to those who sought to fit in with His plan.

I suddenly realized that God was the key to the puzzle of life. Without Him, everything was fragmented, with no real plan or purpose to it. When He was placed properly in the picture, things that had previously been unconnected bits of information suddenly fell into place.

I began to see history, for example, not as a never-ending cycle of unrelated events, but the unfolding of God's plan, with a specific direction and reasons for what, when, why, where and how things happened. I had always wanted my life to have meaning and purpose, and I saw that as I fit into God's plan for life and history, as opposed to trying to set up my own plan, then my life would take on great significance.

That night as I talked with Conrad, I made a conscious decision to actively seek God and His will for my life. Since that time, I've seen Him work to significantly increase the amount of love I have for other people, the amount of joy and peace I experience in the midst of difficult times, the amount of self-control I have to overcome negative habits and patterns of behavior, the amount of wisdom I am able to draw upon to make important decisions, and the amount of enthusiasm and sense of expectation I have as I look forward to what the future holds.

A SUPERIOR WAY OF LIFE

What I first began to see then, and what has been confirmed to me countless times since, is that God is real and offers people a superior way of life. His plan calls for us to be truly happy and truly successful. But the happiness and success He desires is somewhat different than what we generally seek.

For example, the Bible talks about the "fruit of the Spirit" belonging to those who walk in obedience to Him. That fruit is love, joy, peace, patience, kindness, goodness, faithfulness, gentleness, and self-control. Power for living, freedom from fear, wisdom, and purpose are all mentioned as gifts from God to those who follow Him.

Because God is infinite and we are finite, He looks at things from a long-range, eternal perspective. We generally look at things from a short-range, temporal perspective. Very often, the thing that will make us truly happy and truly successful is just the opposite of what we naturally think.

When someone strikes us or insults us, our natural inclination as human beings is to strike them back or insult them in return. God knows, however, that the best way to respond is by showing kindness instead. Jesus says to turn the other cheek if someone strikes you.[191] The Apostle Peter told his readers not to return evil for evil or insult for insult, but to give a blessing instead.[192] The book of Proverbs explains that a soft answer turns away wrath, but a harsh word stirs up strife.[193] God knows that returning evil for evil only leads to greater conflict. The old saying, "You have to fight fire with fire!" is not actually true. You fight fire with water. In the same way, you fight hatred with love.

As finite human beings, we tend to think that greatness is characterized by being above everyone else and telling others what to do. God says, however, that whoever wants to become great among you must be a servant.[194] Most entrepreneurs will tell you that the most successful businesses in a free enterprise system are the ones that best serve their clients – by offering a more efficient or more effective product or service, a better price, or in some other way serving the public better than the competition.

We often think that the way to gain admiration is to cover up our mistakes and failures, and pretend to be someone we are not. God says, "Woe to you ... hypocrites!"[195] And "Before honor comes humility."[196] I've offended a lot of people in my lifetime. But in almost every case where I've gone to them personally and admitted that I was wrong, the people have warmed right up and expressed admiration for the fact that I was willing to acknowledge my error.

The worldly set of values which we follow says that attraction depends on outward appearance. God says, "Let not your adornment be external only. . . But let it be the hidden person of the heart, with the imperishable quality of a gentle and quiet spirit."[197] How many people do you know who fear getting old because their appearance will grow less attractive? My wife is a very attractive woman. However, the qualities that drew me to her were the "imperishable" inner qualities of life that she demonstrated – her kindness, wisdom and maturity – that have only become more attractive with age.

THE MOST DIFFICULT THING IN LIFE

I have become convinced that God is, indeed, real and offers us a superior way of life. But I'm also aware of the fact that He requires from us the most difficult thing in life. He wants us to trust Him, submit our wills to Him and walk in accordance with *His* plan for our lives in place of our own. That is a primary reason why many people don't want to follow Him. They think *their* plan is better than His. It's often the case that people will not turn to God until they have come to a very low point in life where they see clearly that they have really messed things up on their own.

DC, MARVEL ... AND THE BIBLE!

I've often asked people who have had a life-changing encounter with God what it was that initially motivated them to seek to know God. I've obviously received a variety of different answers.

Sometimes, a person will mention an aspect of the quality of life that God offers. For example, that He gave them a sense of purpose in a world that seemed to have no direction. Or He provided a solid source of security at a time in their lives when everything else was falling apart. Sometimes they'll mention the example of a friend or acquaintance who demonstrated an inner strength or quality of life that impressed them. Sometimes they'll mention that Biblical Christianity provided clear answers to questions about life and the world around them that had a ring of truth to them.

For me, it was a desire for significance.

When I was a teenager, I loved to read super-
hero comic books. I was inspired by the exploits of
Superman, Batman, the Fantastic Four, the X-Men,
Captain America, Atom, Aquaman, Daredevil, Flash,
Dr. Strange and others. Then, after I became interest-
ed in following God, my interest turned to the Bible.

I wondered what it was that the two had in common until I realized that superheroes fight cosmic battles between good and evil. I identified with various
comic book characters who had supernatural powers
along with personal issues in their own lives. But they
weren't real. And the villains they fought against
weren't real. They existed only in the imagination.

As a follower of the God of the universe, however, I get to participate in a *real* cosmic battle between
good and evil. I am a *real* superhero ... who fights
real battles ... with *real* spiritual forces at work in the
heavenly and earthly realms.

I've seen God provide for specific needs in my life,
often in amazing ways. And I've also experienced
difficult times where I struggled to make ends meet,
or was misunderstood and mistreated specifically
because of my beliefs. However, God has consistently
stood with me and provided the strength, wisdom
and grace I needed to get through them.

That's what happens when superheroes are called
to serve.

SEARCHING FOR TRUTH

I have become convinced that God *is* real. But He is not Santa Claus ... nor a Divine Watchmaker ... nor a super powerful Genie who attends to our every wish. He is who He says He is – the sovereign Creator and Lord of all things, who alone is truly good. He has communicated with mankind in a way that we can understand. And at a specific point in history, He entered time and space in order to provide a way for us to ultimately enter into His presence to experience fullness of joy.

In Vegas, we encounter an unproven concept. In Hollywood, we encounter the philosophical speculations of finite men. In Bethlehem, we encounter the God of heaven who is, as He said He was, the Way, the Truth and the Life.

ACKNOWLEDGEMENTS

As Christian working in the media industry in the Boston and New York City metropolitan areas for over 40 years, I've had many meaningful conversations with actors, producers, directors, engineers, studio owners and many others about whether or not God is real and the Bible is true.

Some told me they clearly didn't believe in God, thought the Bible was filled with fairy tales and wondered how I could possibly think that a Supreme Being did, in fact, exist. Others weren't sure. They thought there might be a God, but had never heard any clear arguments supporting that belief from what they were taught in school, what they saw or heard in museums and on TV or in conversations with friends and peers. Still others considered themselves believers, but had honest questions that about their faith, and especially why a good God would allow pain and suffering to exist in the world.

Often during those conversations, I wished I had a relatively short, easy-to-read book that I could give them. Not finding any that I liked, I decided to write this one. I am truly grateful for people who have helped make it a reality.

Conrad Koch, the person to whom this book is dedicated and who I talked about in the last chapter, is the person God used to change the direction of my life. Conrad passed away last year. I will be forever grateful for how God used him in my life. If it weren't for him, this book would never have been written.

My wife, Suzan, has always been my greatest supporter. Her encouragement and prayers for me throughout over 50 years of marriage have been instrumental in who I am. As I wrote in a poem many years ago, without her, "I would never have learned how to fly!"

Jack Linn was my roommate in college and the editor of my first book, *Heaven's Doors ... Wider Than You Ever Believed!* He's the kind of editor most authors wished they had. His comments, suggestions and advice made this book so much better than what it would have been without him.

I worked with Debbi Stocco when I needed some help with eBook formatting for my earlier book and a subsequent booklet. Her skill and creativity prompted me to ask her to design and typeset the interior of this book. I'm grateful for her excellent work.

When Steve Kuhn sent me the first draft of the cover he designed, it was clearly different from what I had been thinking of ... but so much better than what I had been thinking of. He also suggested I make some subtle changes to the title and subtitle. I quickly saw that his advice was well worth listening to and followed it. Thank you, Steve.

Receiving an unsolicited endorsement from Christian elder statesman, lawyer, professor theologian and author John Warwick Montgomery was a great encouragement. He was gracious enough to read through my manuscript and even pass my name on to a publisher. I am grateful!

I'm also grateful for the artistic expertise and encouragement of Fred Daunno.

Thank You, God, for these wonderful people!

WHAT HAPPENS AFTER WE DIE?

For the first 500 years after Christ, most Christians believed that God would ultimately redeem all of His creation. They believed Hell was real, but it doesn't last forever. Its purpose is to restore, not just to punish.

Heaven's Doors by George W. Sarris explains both historically and Biblically how Jesus Christ succeeded in His mission to seek and save the lost. And it shows how the doors to heaven really are wider than you ever believed!

Available in paperback, eBook and audiobook formats from Amazon.com.

ENDNOTES

1. "Gargarin was a baptized faithful throughout all his life," says General Valentin Petrov, Professor of the Russian Air Force Academy and a personal friend of the cosmonaut. "He always confessed God whenever he was provoked, no matter where he was." - https://www.beliefnet.com/columnists/on_the_front_lines_of_the_culture_wars/2011/04/yuri-gagarin-first-human-in-space-was-a-devout-christian-says-his-close-friend.html; https://www.businessinsider.com/strange-connection-between-russian-astronauts-and-god-2014-7

2. The most prominent cosmonaut atheist was Gherman Titov whose flight in August 1961 followed Yuri Gargarin's earlier April flight. He told an audience at the Seattle World's Fair in 1962 that he had seen no gods or angels in space, and that he believed in mankind's strength and reason. Some suggest the "There Is No God!" poster commemorates him. - https://www.theguardian.com/artanddesign/gallery/2019/oct/23/down-with-god-how-the-soviet-union-took-on-religion-in-pictures

3. https://en.wikipedia.org/wiki/Apollo_8_Genesis_reading

4. https://exoplanets.nasa.gov/what-is-an-exoplanet/what-is-the-universe/; https://www.thefactsite.com/100-space-facts/; https://sky-andtelescope.org/astronomy-resources/how-many-stars-are-there/

5. https://www.universetoday.com/15220/are-the-laws-of-nature-the-same-everywhere-in-the-universe/. For example, research conducted by an international team of astronomers shows that one of the most important numbers in physics theory, the proton-electron mass ratio, is almost exactly the same in a galaxy 6 billion light years away as it is in Earth's laboratories, approximately 1836.15.

6. Ecclesiastes 1:14

7. https://en.wikipedia.org/wiki/Buzz_Aldrin

8. https://kidadl.com/articles/clarence-darrow-quotes-from-the-famous-american-lawyer

9. https://www.history.com/this-day-in-history/monkey-trial-begins; https://en.wikipedia.org/wiki/Scopes_Trial

10. For more information on Intelligent Design, see Discovery Institute FAQs - https://www.discovery.org/id/faqs/. For information on Creation Science, see Answers in Genesis – https://answersingenesis.org/

11. https://rationalwiki.org/wiki/Lists_of_creationist_scientists

12. This Law is also known as the 2nd Law of Thermodynamics – For more information, see LibreTexts – https://chem.libretexts.org/Textbook_Maps/Physical_and_Theoretical_Chemistry_Textbook_Maps/Supplemental_Modules_(Physical_and_Theoretical_Chemistry)/Thermodynamics/The_Four_Laws_of_Thermodynamics/Second_Law_of_Thermodynamics. See also, Lumen, *Introduction to Chemistry*, The Three Laws of Thermodynamics – https://courses.lumenlearning.com/introchem/chapter/the-three-laws-of-thermodynamics/

13. Cf. Jonathan Sarfati, PhD, FM, *Refuting Evolution*, Chapter 3 – https://creation.com/refuting-evolution-chapter-3-the-links-are-missing

14. Cf. Casey Luskin, *Problem 5: Abrupt Appearance of Species in the Fossil Record Does Not Support Darwinian Evolution*, Evolution News & Science Today – https://evolutionnews.org/2015/01/problem_5_abrup/.

15. Cf. Lanny Johnson, *Sea Anemone & Sea Slug* – http://www.discovercreation.org/kids/amazing-creatures/sea-anemone-sea-slug/; Matt Simon, *Absurd Creature of the Week: This Crazy-Looking Sea Slug Has An Ingenious Secret Weapon* – https://www.wired.com/2014/11/absurd-creature-week-nudibranch-sea-slug/; Jessica Goodheart, *How Sea Slugs Steal the Defenses of their Prey* – https://ocean.si.edu/ocean-life/invertebrates/how-sea-slugs-steal-defenses-their-prey

16. The question about the monkeys actually draws attention to additional questions that evolutionists need to answer. Where did the monkeys come from? Monkeys are actually living creatures with the strength and manual dexterity necessary to push typewriter keys. They are, in effect, intelligent and skillful designers. As it relates to

the question of Evolution, "chance" alone is not sufficient to bring together all of the key elements necessary for the formation of life from non-living elements. Where did the typewriters come from? Typewriters are sophisticated machines with carefully designed, inter-locking parts working precisely together. A question for Evolution is how did the sophisticated chemical processes that enable substances to combine in unique ways originate? Where did the language come from? Language shows evidence of a phenomenally complex design, encoding a tremendous amount of information. Similar to the way the order of letters in the alphabet can be used to form a word, the order of nitrogen bases in a DNA sequence forms genes, which are the instruction manuals for life. – Rachael Rettner, *What is DNA?*, LiveScience, https://www.livescience.com/37247-dna.html; Corey Binns, *Genes: The Instruction Manuals for Life*, LiveScience, https://www.livescience.com/10486-genes-instruction-manuals-life.html

17. https://www.yourdictionary.com/theory

18. https://en.wikipedia.org/wiki/Star_Wars

19. https://en.wikipedia.org/wiki/The_Force

20. George Lucas during a production meeting for *The Empire Strikes Back* – https://en.wikipedia.org/wiki/The_Force

21. Obi-Wan Kenobi in *Star Wars* Episode IV, *A New Hope* – https://en.wikiquote.org/wiki/The_Force

22. The focus was on energy, because Albert Einstein's Theory of Special Relativity concluded that mass and energy are really the same physical entity. That was demonstrated conclusively with the con-struction of the first atomic bomb. About 2.2 pounds of uranium-235 released an amount of energy equivalent to over 15,000 tons of TNT, achieving temperatures of several million degrees in the explod-ing bomb itself. – *Atomic Bomb*, Editors of Encyclopedia Brittanica, https://www.britannica.com/technology/atomic-bomb

23. James Ashenhurst, *What Holds the Nucleus Together?*, Master Organic Chemistry, December 21, 2019, https://www.masterorganic-chemistry.com/2010/07/16/what-holds-the-nucleus-together/#:~:-text=The%20strong%20nuclear%20force.,their%20charges%20repel%20each%20other.: see also, https://www.britannica.com/sci-ence/subatomic-particle/Stable-and-resonant-hadrons

24. Colossians 1:16

25. Corinne Yee (UCD), Desiree Rozzi (UCD), LibreTexts, *Unusual Properties of Water,* https://chem.libretexts.org/Textbook_Maps/Physical_and_Theoretical_Chemistry_Textbook_Maps/Supplemental_Modules_(Physical_and_Theoretical_Chemistry)/Physical_Properties_of_Matter/States_of_Matter/Properties_of_Liquids/Unusual_Properties_of_Water

26. *Human Genetic Potential,* Functional Chiropractic, https://www.funchiropractic.com/human-genetic-potential/#:~:text=This%20information%20is%20coded%20into,half%20this%20amount%20of%20DNA.)&text=As%20a%20carrier%20of%20information,skilled%20teams%20of%20design%20engineers. See also, http://www.esalq.usp.br/lepse/imgs/conteudo_thumb/The-Complexity-of-the-Cell.pdf

27. *Bombadier Beetle,* https://en.wikipedia.org/wiki/Bombardier_beetle

28. https://www.theguardian.com/books/2011/dec/16/christopher-hitchens-obituary

29. https://en.wikipedia.org/wiki/Christopher_Hitchens#Books

30. Bruce DeSilva, https://en.wikipedia.org/wiki/God_Is_Not_Great

31. Kabir Helminski, https://en.wikipedia.org/wiki/God_Is_Not_Great

32. https://www.bbc.com/news/uk-16212418

33. BBC, *Religions, Hinduism,* https://www.bbc.co.uk/religion/religions/hinduism/#:~:text=Hinduism%20is%20the%20religion%20of,commonly%20agreed%20set%20of%20teachings.

34. *Zoroastrianism,* https://en.wikipedia.org/wiki/Zoroastrianism

35. *Shinto,* Oxford Dictionary

36. https://asiasociety.org/education/shinto

37. *Taoism,* National Geographic, https://www.nationalgeographic.org/encyclopedia/taoism/

38. *Tao Te Ching,* https://en.wikipedia.org/wiki/Tao_Te_Ching

39. *Jainism,* Oxford Dictionary

40. BBC, *Religions, Jainism, https://www.bbc.co.uk/religion/religions/ jainism/ataglance/glance.shtml*

41. Cf. *Buddhism, https://en.wikipedia.org/wiki/Buddhism; Gautama Buddha, https://en.wikipedia.org/wiki/Gautama_Buddha;* History. com, *Buddhism,* https://www.history.com/topics/religion/buddhism#:~:text=Followers%20of%20Buddhism%20don't,man%2C%20 but%20not%20a%20god.

42. *Confucianism,* National Geographic, https://www.nationalgeographic.org/encyclopedia/confucianism/

43. *Quran,* https://en.wikipedia.org/wiki/Quran

44. *God in Islam,* https://en.wikipedia.org/wiki/God_in_Islam

45. *God in Mormonism,* https://en.wikipedia.org/wiki/God_in_Mormonism#:~:text=The%20Book%20of%20Mormon%20teaches,speaking%20as%20a%20man%20would.

46. *Mormonism and Polygamy,* https://en.wikipedia.org/wiki/Mormonism_and_polygamy

47. *WorldCat,* the WorldCat union catalog, https://en.wikipedia.org/ wiki/WorldCat

48. Cf. Wycliffe Bible Translators, https://www.wycliffe.org.uk/about/ our-impact/

49. *Bibles Printed and Sold,* Christian Research, https://www.christian-research.org/reports/archives-and-statistics/the-bible/

50. The Gideons International, https://www.gideons.org/about

51. *The Gideons International,* https://en.wikipedia.org/wiki/ The_Gideons_International#:~:text=Members%20of%20The%20 Gideons%20International,distributed%20over%20two%20billion%20 Bibles.

52. James Clear, https://jamesclear.com/best-books/best-selling

53. https://www.dictionary.com/browse/unique

54. https://en.wikipedia.org/wiki/Croesus

55. https://en.wikipedia.org/wiki/Pythia

56. https://www.historyanswers.co.uk/ancient/cleopatras-affairs-were-a-political-gamble-that-failed/

57. https://en.wikipedia.org/wiki/Pythia

58. https://en.wikipedia.org/wiki/List_of_oracular_statements_from_Delphi

59. Matthew 5:18

60. II Peter 1:20-21

61. II Timothy 3:16-17

62. Isaiah 41:21-23; 42:8-9

63. Randolf S. Foster, *Studies in Theology, Evidences of Christianity, The Supernatural Book*, Hunt & Easton, 1890, p. 111

64. Deuteronomy 18:21-22

65. Deuteronomy 13:1-2, 5

66. Archeologist and author Patrick Hunt, https://en.wikipedia.org/wiki/Cyrus_the_Great

67. Isaiah 44: 24-28; 45:1-3

68. Ezra 1:2-4

69. Cyrus Cylinder, Lines 30-35 - http://www.britishmuseum.org/explore/highlights/article_index/c/cyrus_cylinder_-_translation.aspx

70. Herodotus, *Histories*, Book I, 178-186

71. *Babylon*, Encyclopedia Britannica, 1911- http://www.1911encyclopedia.org/Babylon

72. *Walls of Babylon* - http://www.globalsecurity.org/military/world/iraq/babylon-walls.htm

73. Jeremiah 51:53

74. Isaiah 13:17-22

75. See http://en.wikipedia.org/wiki/Babylon

76. Herodotus, *Histories*, Book I, 191 – "Cyrus was now reduced to great perplexity, as time went on and he made no progress against the place. In this distress either some one made the suggestion to

him, or he bethought himself of a plan, which he proceeded to put in execution ... he turned the Euphrates by a canal into the basin, which was then a marsh, on which the river sank to such an extent that the natural bed of the stream became fordable.

Hereupon the Persians who had been left for the purpose at Babylon by the river-side, entered the stream, which had now sunk so as to reach about midway up a man's thigh, and thus got into the town ... the Persians came upon them by surprise and so took the city. Owing to the vast size of the place, the inhabitants of the central parts (as the residents at Babylon declare) long after the outer portions of the town were taken, knew nothing of what had chanced, but as they were engaged in a festival, continued dancing and reveling until they learnt about the capture. Such, then, were the circumstances of the first taking of Babylon."

77. https://www.britannica.com/biography/Belshazzar; Daniel, chapter 5. For information on the identity of Darius the Mede, see https://truthonlybible.com/2016/01/08/darius-the-mede-a-solution-to-his-identity/

78. Daniel 5:25-28

79. For further information, see Paul Ferguson PhD, *Ezekiel 26:1-14: A Proof Text For Inerrancy or Fallibility of The Old Testament?*, https://biblearchaeology.org/research/chronological-categories/babylonian-exile-persian-period/3304-ezekiel-26114-a-proof-text-for-inerrancy-or-fallibility-of-the-old-testament?highlight=WyJ0eXJlIiwidHlyZSdzIiwidHlyZSciXQ==

80. Ezekiel 26:3-4, 12-14

81. Cf. https://www.britannica.com/biography/Julius-Wellhausen

82. https://en.wikipedia.org/wiki/Hittites

83. https://www.newsweek.com/did-it-happen-178962

84. https://biblicalarchaeologygraves.blogspot.com/2014/12/bonus-14-mari-tablets.html

85. https://www.newsweek.com/did-it-happen-178962

86. https://en.wikipedia.org/wiki/Tel_Dan_stele

87. https://en.wikipedia.org/wiki/Philistines#cite_note-3

88. https://en.wikipedia.org/wiki/Cylinders_of_Nabonidus#cite_note-1. The Nabonidus Cylinder from Ur states:

"As for me, Nabonidus, king of Babylon, save me from sinning against your great godhead and grant me as a present a life long of days, and as for Belshazzar, the eldest son -my offspring- instill reverence for your great godhead in his heart and may he not commit any cultic mistake, may he be sated with a life of plenitude." - https://www.livius.org/sources/content/nabonidus-cylinder-from-ur/

89. https://whygodreallyexists.com/archives/archaeology-confirms-the-bible

90. https://web.archive.org/web/20110718171841/http://chesterrep.openrepository.com/cdr/bitstream/10034/40813/1/Some%20Notes%20on%20Crucifixion.pdf

91. https://en.wikipedia.org/wiki/Caiaphas_ossuary

92. https://en.wikipedia.org/wiki/Gamaliel; Acts 5:38-39, The Voice

93. https://www.britannica.com/biography/Bar-Kokhba-Jewish-leader

94. https://en.wikipedia.org/wiki/Simon_bar_Kokhba

95. https://www.britannica.com/biography/Bar-Kokhba-Jewish-leader; https://en.wikipedia.org/wiki/Simon_bar_Kokhba

96. Genesis 3:15

97. Genesis 12:1-3 – *"The LORD had said to Abram, 'Leave your country, your people and your father's household and go to the land I will show you. I will make you into a great nation and I will bless you; I will make your name great, and you will be a blessing. I will bless those who bless you, and whoever curses you I will curse; and all peoples on earth will be blessed through you.'"*

98. Genesis 21:12 – *"But God said to him, 'Do not be so distressed about the boy and your maidservant. Listen to whatever Sarah tells you, because it is through Isaac that your offspring will be reckoned.'"*

99. Genesis 25:23 – *God said to Rebekah, Isaac's wife, "Two nations are in your womb, and two peoples from within you will be separated; one people will be stronger than the other, and the older will serve the younger."*

100. Genesis 49:10 – *"The scepter will not depart from Judah, nor the ruler's staff from between his feet, until he comes to whom it belongs and the obedience of the nations is his."*

101. II Samuel 7:12-13

102. Micah 5:2, 4-5a

103. Genesis 49:10

104. Daniel 9:24-27 – *"Seventy 'sevens' are decreed for your people and your holy city to finish transgression, to put an end to sin, to atone for wickedness, to bring in everlasting righteousness, to seal up vision and prophecy and to anoint the most holy. Know and understand this: From the issuing of the decree to restore and rebuild Jerusalem until the Anointed One, the ruler, comes, there will be seven 'sevens,' and sixty-two 'sevens.' It will be rebuilt with streets and a trench, but in times of trouble. After the sixty-two 'sevens,' the Anointed One will be cut off and will have nothing. The people of the ruler who will come will destroy the city and the sanctuary. The end will come like a flood: War will continue until the end, and desolations have been decreed. He will confirm a covenant with many for one 'seven.' In the middle of the 'seven' he will put an end to sacrifice and offering. And on a wing of the temple he will set up an abomination that causes desolation, until the end that is decreed is poured out on him."*

An excellent exposition of this prophecy and critique of various interpretations can be found in *A Dissertation on the Prophecy Contained in Daniel IX:24-27*, published in 1811 by Rev. George Stanley Faber , London, F.C. and J Rivington - http://books.google.com/books?id=dNs7AAAAcAAJ&pg=PA5&dq=Dissertation+on+Daniel's+-seventy+weeks&hl=en&sa=X&ei=aGu-T4q9FKr26AG5oYEg&ved=0CG-cQ6AEwBQ#v=onepage&q=Dissertation%20on%

105. For a free download of the book from Google Books, go to - http://books.google.com/books?id=gG5BAAAAcAAJ&printsec=-frontcover&dq=editions:i9wuUmGvMBYC&hl=en&sa=X&ei=7uuaT-6LtBKT66QHLg9WSDw&ved=0CDAQ6AEwAA#v=onepage&q=edi-tions%3Ai9wuUmGvMBYC&f=false

106. The Biblical book of Ezra states that Ezra began his journey from Babylon to rebuild Jerusalem on the first day of the first month of

the seventh year of Artaxerxes in Ezra 7:7-9. Newton had an extensive knowledge of ancient history. He identified the Persian king as Artaxerxes I (Longimanus) and placed the decree in the year 458 BC. Depending on whether the prophecy began when Ezra left Babylon or when he arrived in Jerusalem and started building, Newton offered two dates for the endpoint – AD 33 or AD 34. When calculating the number of years from 458 BC to AD 33, it is important to note that there was no 0 BC. The year AD 1 followed 1 BC.

"Here, by putting a week for seven years, are reckoned 490 years from the time that the dispersed Jews should be re-incorporated into a people and a holy city, until the death and resurrection of Christ; whereby transgression should be finished, and sins ended, iniquity be expiated, and everlasting righteousness be brought in, and this Vision be accomplished, and the Prophet (Newton translated this as "Prophet" rather than "prophecy" and understood it as referring specifically to Christ) consummated, that Prophet whom the Jews expected; and whereby the most Holy should be anointed, he who is therefore in the next words called the Anointed, that is, the Messiah, or the Christ."
- Sir Isaac Newton, *Observations upon the Prophecies of Daniel and the Apocalypse of St. John*, Part 1, J. Darby and T. Browne, London, 1733, p. 130. http://books.google.com/books?id=gG5BAAAAcAA-J&printsec=frontcover&dq=editions:i9wuUmGvMBYC&hl=en&sa=X-&ei=7uuaT6LtBKT66QHLg9WSDw&ved=0CDAQ6AEwAA#v=onepage&q=editions%3Ai9wuUmGvMBYC&f

107. The other date is Friday April 7, AD 30. The early date is chosen by those who believe that Herod's death occurred in 4 or 3 BC, making the birth of Jesus in 4 or 3 BC. However, other scholarly evidence indicates that Herod died in the year 1 BC, making the date of Friday April 3, AD 33 the correct date of the crucifixion. For a discussion of the dates, see Biblical History Daily, November 30, 2020 - https://www.biblicalarchaeology.org/daily/people-cultures-in-the-bible/jesus-historical-jesus/herods-death-jesus-birth-and-a-lunar-eclipse/

108. Isaiah 7:14; 9:6-7

109. Jeremiah 22:28-30

110. Isaiah 53:1-12 – *"Who has believed our message and to whom has the arm of the LORD been revealed? He grew up before him like a tender shoot, and like a root out of dry ground. He had no beauty or majesty to attract us to him, nothing in his appearance that we*

should desire him. He was despised and rejected by men, a man of sorrows, and familiar with suffering. Like one from whom men hide their faces he was despised, and we esteemed him not.

Surely he took up our infirmities and carried our sorrows, yet we considered him stricken by God, smitten by him, and afflicted. But he was pierced for our transgressions, he was crushed for our iniquities; the punishment that brought us peace was upon him, and by his wounds we are healed. We all, like sheep, have gone astray, each of us has turned to his own way; and the LORD has laid on him the iniquity of us all.

He was oppressed and afflicted, yet he did not open his mouth; he was led like a lamb to the slaughter, and as a sheep before her shearers is silent, so he did not open his mouth. By oppression and judgment he was taken away.

And who can speak of his descendants? For he was cut off from the land of the living; for the transgression of my people he was stricken. He was assigned a grave with the wicked, and with the rich in his death, though he had done no violence, nor was any deceit in his mouth.

Yet it was the LORD's will to crush him and cause him to suffer, and though the LORD makes his life a guilt offering, he will see his offspring and prolong his days, and the will of the LORD will prosper in his hand. After the suffering of his soul, he will see the light of life and be satisfied; by his knowledge my righteous servant will justify many, and he will bear their iniquities. Therefore I will give him a portion among the great, and he will divide the spoils with the strong, because he poured out his life unto death, and was numbered with the transgressors. For he bore the sin of many, and made intercession for the transgressors."

111. https://bookriot.com/10-things-you-should-know-about-the-gutenberg-bible/

112. In 1999, the A&E Network ranked Gutenberg no. 1 on their "People of the Millennium" countdown

113. https://en.wikipedia.org/wiki/Johannes_Gutenberg; https://bookriot.com/10-things-you-should-know-about-the-gutenberg-bible/

114. Revelation, 22:18-19

115. https://israelmyglory.org/article/the-ancient-sopherim/

116. https://israelmyglory.org/article/the-ancient-sopherim/

117. https://en.wikipedia.org/wiki/Masoretes#:~:text=The%20Mas-oretes%20(Hebrew%3A%20%D7%91%D7%A2%D7%9C%D7%99%20%D7%94%D7%9E%D7%A1%D7%95%D7%A8%D7%94,as%20in%20 Iraq%20(Babylonia).

118. Cf. https://riverviewbc.com/wp-content/uploads/Jewish-and-Masoretic-Rules-for-Copying-the-Scripture.pdf

119. https://apologeticspress.org/apPubPage.aspx?pub=1&is-sue=444

120. https://truthfaithandreason.com/case-making-101-how-does-the-bible-compare-to-other-ancient-documents/.

These numbers increase with ongoing discoveries in archeology. The numbers in this article were thanks to Karl Udy and Dr. Clay Jones of Biola University as of 2013.

121. https://en.wikipedia.org/wiki/Biblical_manuscript#:~:tex-t=The%20New%20Testament%20has%20been,%2C%20Ethiop-ic%2C%20Coptic%20and%20Armenian; https://truthfaithandreason.com/case-making-101-how-does-the-bible-compare-to-other-an-cient-documents/

122. https://truthfaithandreason.com/case-making-101-how-does-the-bible-compare-to-other-ancient-documents/

123. https://web.archive.org/web/20090621000932/http://www.time.com/time/magazine/article/0,9171,905202-1,00.html

124. https://en.wikipedia.org/wiki/Explo_%2772

125. https://en.wikipedia.org/wiki/Explo_%2772

126. https://web.archive.org/web/20090621000932/http://www.time.com/time/magazine/article/0,9171,905202-1,00.html

127. https://www.yourdictionary.com/evil

128. Cf. https://us.norton.com/products?inid=nortoncom_nav_prod-ucts_internetsecurity:malware-what-is-a-computer-virus

129. https://www.pewforum.org/2019/10/17/in-u-s-decline-of-christianity-continues-at-rapid-pace/

130. https://www.deseret.com/indepth/2021/3/24/22348276/the-power-of-one-religious-nones-unaffiliated-atheist-agnostic-belief-in-god

131. https://www.pewforum.org/2019/10/17/in-u-s-decline-of-christianity-continues-at-rapid-pace/

132. https://www.northjersey.com/in-depth/news/2021/09/20/nones-religiously-unaffiliated-americans-increasing/4386549001/

133. https://news.gallup.com/opinion/polling-matters/267920/millennials-religiosity-amidst-rise-nones.aspx

134. https://en.wikipedia.org/wiki/Emergency_workers_killed_in_the_September_11_attacks. 343 were firefighters, including a chaplain and two paramedics, of the New York City Fire Department; 37 were police officers of the Port Authority of New York and New Jersey Police Department; 23 were police officers of the New York City Police Department; 8 were emergency medical technicians and paramedics from private emergency medical services; and 1 was a patrolman from the New York Fire Patrol.

135. Genesis 1:26-27

136. https://en.wikipedia.org/wiki/The_Holocaust

137. Romans 3:10-12

138. Mark 7:21-23

139. I John 4:19

140. Deuteronomy 6:4

141. Isaiah 45:5-6, 21-22

142. Genesis 1:26

143. Genesis 3:22

144. John 1:1

145. Philippians 2:6-8

146. John G. Paton, James Paton; *John G. Paton Missionary to the New Hebrides, An Autobiography* edited by his brother James Paton, 1889, 1898, First Banner of Truth Trust edition,1965, Reprinted 1994, p. 72

147. Matthew 11:28; John 14:6; 10:30; 14:9; 6:35; 7:37-38; 8:12; 10:14; 11:25

148. *Ozymandias* – by Percy Bysshe Shelley

I met a traveler from an antique land
Who said: "Two vast and trunkless legs of stone
Stand in the desert ... Near them, on the sand,
Half sunk, a shattered visage lies, whose frown,
And wrinkled lip, and sneer of cold command,
Tell that its sculptor well those passions read
Which yet survive, stamped on these lifeless things,
The hand that mocked them, and the heart that fed:
And on the pedestal these words appear:
'My name is Ozymandias, king of kings:
Look on my works, ye Mighty, and despair!'
Nothing beside remains. Round the decay
Of that colossal wreck, boundless and bare
The lone and level sands stretch far away."

149. https://www.newworldencyclopedia.org/entry/Ramesses_II

150. https://en.wikipedia.org/wiki/Ozymandias

151. https://www.thecollector.com/ramesses-the-great-warrior-builder-and-divine-king/

152. https://en.wikipedia.org/wiki/Ramesses_II

153. https://www.dailysabah.com/opinion/columns/who-does-the-single-grave-in-the-tomb-of-prophet-muhammad-belong-to

154. https://en.wikipedia.org/wiki/Cemetery_of_Confucius

155. https://en.wikipedia.org/wiki/List_of_purported_relics_of_major_figures_of_religious_traditions ; https://en.wikipedia.org/wiki/Gautama_Buddha#Last_days_and_parinirvana

156. John 9:32

157. I Corinthians 15:14-15, 17,19

158. Luke 18:31-33

159. I Corinthians 15:3-8

160. Matthew 28:12-14

161. Acts 4:13

162. https://en.wikipedia.org/wiki/Albert_Henry_Ross

163. Frank Morison, *Who Moved the Stone?*, Preface and p. 192. First published in 1930 by Faber and Faber Limited; Interv-Varsity Press edition, 1969

164. Job 2:7; Samuel J. Schultz, *The Old Testament Speaks*, Harper & Row, Second Edition, 1960 & 1970, p. 280

165. Job 1:8; 2:3

166. Deuteronomy 20:16-17

167. New England Journal of Medicine, 324, March 7, 1991, pp. 691-694.

168. *When Is It Right To Die?*, Joni Eareckson, Zondervan, 1992, p. 169

169. December 23, 1997 edition

170. *Scars & Stripes*, by Eugene B. McDaniel, pp. 37, 39

171. Job 38:2, The Living Bible

172. Job 42:3, 5 NASB

173. Proverbs chapter 3, verses 13-18

174. *Scars & Stripes*, p. 39

175. Dr. Jack van Hoff, MD, personal correspondence

176. Dr. Ezekiel J. Emmanuel, Lead Author, Dana-Farber Cancer Institute Survey, published in Lancet, June 29, 1996

177. II Corinthians 11:23-27

178. Romans 5:3-5

179. Natalie Angier, The New York Times, *Joined for Life, and Living Life to the Full,* December 23, 1997

180. After winning the award, Reba changed her name to George. As of 2022, both twins are still living.

181. Eugene B. McDaniel, *Scars & Stripes,* Harvest House Publishers, 1975, p. 167

182. Eugene B. McDaniel, *Scars & Stripes,* Harvest House Publishers, 1975, *169*

183. Philippians 1:12-14

184. Robyn Stecher

185. Genesis 6:5-7

186. Isaiah 57:1-2

187. John 14:2, King James Version

188. *Heaven's Doors ... Wider Than You Ever Believed!,* George W. Sarris, GWS Publishing, 2017. The book is available as a paperback, eBook or audiobook on Amazon.com – https://www.amazon.com/Heavens-Doors-Wider-Than-Believed/dp/0980085322/ref=tmm_pap_swatch_0?_encoding=UTF8&qid=1635359394&sr=8-1

189. Howard Rutledge, *In the Presence of Mine Enemies,* Spire Books, 1975, pp. 70, 93

190. The person who asked that question was Conrad Koch, the man to whom this book is dedicated.

191. Matthew 5:39

192. I Peter 3:9

193. Proverbs 15:1

194. Matthew 20:26

195. Matthew 23:13ff

196. Proverbs 15:33

197. I Peter 3:3-4